Chainsaws and Cherry Burls

Essays and Vignettes

Jennifer Neves

Praise for *Chainsaws and Cherry Burls*

"An enjoyable peek into a chaotic but wildly fascinating family and their life on a farm in rural Maine. This smart and loving group captures our interest in the same way the natural world captures theirs. Filled with hilarious escapades, these pages depict the land teaching both parents and rambunctious children about its deeply held secrets. In a time when transience abounds, this charming family's rootedness to a *place* inspires, as does their devotion to each other. Prepare to be awed as you explore with this relatable lot."

Linda MacKillop, author of *The Forgotten Life of Eva Gordon* and *Hotel Oscar Mike Echo*

"While reading Jennifer Neves' *Chainsaws and Cherry Burls*, I fell in love with her family. Her husband and baby, her children, all of them, actually, one at a time, and, of course, with Jennifer and her wide-open amazing world. This family's Maine farm life is busy, wonderful, chaotic, hard, and lovely. It's a life of challenge, experiment, and thoughtfulness. This collection creates a tapestry of connection that explores family, nature, and an evolving relationship between the two. Neves writes with humor, compassion, and tenderness about the days that unfold on 42 acres of orchard and woodland. Leeches, mice, skunks, and madcap adventures coalesce to form a portrait of a family that adores each other and the land. There is beauty in each burl and book read at night to each child. I loved every single word."

Jessica Barksdale Inclán, author of *What the Moon Did* and *Trick of the Porch Light*

Chainsaws and Cherry Burls: Essays and Vignettes

Copyright © 2023 by Jennifer Neves

Cover Design by Fernanda Zanchetta

All rights reserved. No part of this book may be reproduced or transmitted in any form or by any means without written permission of the author.

ISBN 978-1-943424-78-8

LCCN 2022948344

North Country Press
Unity, Maine

For Jack, Bellamy, Ogden, and Ezra

Also by Jennifer Neves

Backpack Like You Mean It

Freedom Farm

Table of Contents

42 Acres 1
The Orchard 8
Leeches 19
Hatchets, Sword Fights, and Water Balloons 26
Today on the Farm: Dada 35
Body and Soil 37
Machinery 45
Woodpile 48
Today on the Farm: Day Eight 53
Snow Day 55
Today on the Farm: Broken Pocket 62
Spa Day 63
For the Birds 68
Today on the Farm: Skunks 72
A Helper 80
Battleground 84
Today on the Farm: Mama is Mad 93
The Art of the Bench 96
Autumn Rain 100
The Bracelet I Wear 102
Chainsaws and Cherry Burls 109
Bellamy's Raccoon 114
Tulip Petunia 120

Going Home 124
Up Here, I Write 133
Today on the Farm: Seedpod 137
What We Leave Behind 139
Acknowledgements 145

42 Acres

Let me introduce myself.

The lilac blossoms are falling. Tiny faded purple flowers cover the ground beneath the bird feeders, like misplaced snowflakes against the green. Spring has come and gone and I'm not sure I will survive another year without having smelled a bouquet of lily of the valley. How did I miss them?

I am a fifty-year-old woman who lives on a 42-acre farm in rural Maine. Well, it *used* to be a farm. The land dips and rises with the weight of the old rock walls as they move in chains like a sine wave from ledgy peaks to the soft gullies of creek beds and ancient roads long washed out by spring rains. What this land is now, I can't say for sure. I am trying to figure it out. It is not lost on me that Douglas Adams famously wrote in *The Hitchhiker's Guide to the Galaxy*, "The answer to the ultimate question of life, the universe, and everything is 42." For this farm and this family, in Adams's cosmic joke there is a seed of truth. There are no crops on our 42 acres. No animals, save myself, my husband, four children, a dog, a snake, a rabbit, and countless unwelcome rodents. There is no agricultural industry to speak of. Despite this, I cannot help myself from answering, "On a farm," when someone asks where I live.

The land here has just begun to speak to me. It didn't when we first moved in four years ago, probably because I was pregnant and tired and still trying to figure out whether we'd made a huge mistake in buying it.

At first, the land felt silent on frigid days when the house windows leaked and my toes went white with cold on the kitchen floor. I didn't hear it in spring when the no-see-ems (the Maine term for tiny biting black flies that manage to sneak through screens and windows without proper seals) showed up, or in early summer when the mosquitos won out, their buzzing a soul-crushing reminder that in Maine, the outdoors does not come free from some form of physical discomfort for most of the year.

In the beginning, I would hear the land whisper once in a while on quiet winter evenings when I put on boots and jacket and snuck from the din of this family farmhouse. Standing in the dark, stars glittering above, I closed my eyes and listened for the call. Though honestly, even in the dead quiet of a winter night, it was so faint I couldn't make out the meaning. I do believe honesty is important, so I should admit that when I say I am fifty, what I mean to say is that I am almost fifty because being in your forties is essentially the same thing as being fifty. It all feels middle-agey and hardly worth the distinction.

~

I believe we are a collection of important truths, that the little things about who we are define us as much as the big things. Maybe more so. Aren't we all an accumulation of a million selves stacked atop one another through time? Which is more important: that I was once run over by a bicycle or that I find cauliflower a truly horrendous vegetable?

These things are neither here nor there. They are both here and there.

I am a person who cannot wear socks that don't match. Although I admire people with the ability to detach themselves from an emotional investment in the color of a sock's heel or toe and how it relates to anther sock's colors, I am not that person. If a sock does not have a mate, it will sit in a basket until one is found or I die.

I am a person who loves to clean things up. If there are sticks in the forest and I am walking past them, I will stack them into a pile to make the forest floor seem tidier.

I am a person who does not enjoy being wet.

I am a person who believes that land is sacred; that we are connected to it in unseen ways and that it feeds our bodies and minds as we move through it.

I am a person who believes in science.

A person who smells smoke when there is no smoke and cannot figure out why but has never bothered to mention this to anyone before writing it just now.

I am a person who always rounds up when it comes to age. And since we're on the topic, I should mention that I am in fact not in my forties. I am actually 39. But being 39 hardly seems a distance from my forties, which are practically midlife and certainly not worth fussing about and so, you see, I rounded. I also always round up when it comes to how long something takes. This quality is one that baffles my husband because he cannot understand why one would round oneself out of youth, out of time. I have tried to explain it, but in truth, I'm just grasping at the tendrils of my own neuroses. Maybe it gives me a false sense of extra time, to realize I am indeed not yet fifty, but have reported to everyone, including myself, that I am practically so. There is a space between reality and perception in which I feel very comfortable. A space in which I am allowed some leeway. I could likely drill into this habit with a therapist but as of yet have chosen not to.

Despite enjoying the dance between perception and reality, I should note that in some cases, there is no wiggle room. These 42 acres will never be 50 acres, or 25.

~

At 39, I keep asking myself the question: What matters? The 42 acres matter.

The lilies of the valley matter. Noticing the way a breeze carries their sweetness after a spring shower. Their tiny white bells hidden in a sea of green on the back hillside beneath the twin birch, leaves just greening out. They matter because they come and they go and this year, I missed them.

Lilies of the valley used to grow beneath a forsythia bush at the old farmhouse in Freedom, Maine, where I grew up. When I was little, I would lay beneath the branches and smell them without picking them, so they might last the whole season. I remember my mother working to prepare her garden while I lay, feeling the spring sun on my face, wishing the sweet smell would last just a little longer. How many times in this life will I smell these intoxicating flowers? How many seasons can I afford to miss because I forgot to pay attention?

I am paying attention now.

This land is a classroom in which to get lost. It is full of questions I am just now waking up to ask. What is this star-shaped flower, white petals peeking through the lily leaves? The eleven-o'clock lady, beauty masking poison in her bulbs. Littering the forest floor, the Canadian mayflower, a shade dweller has been here all along. Strange that I can't remember ever taking the time to pick one to smell it. Today, I did. It was sweeter than I expected. I feel silly to admit my expectations were based on my belief that this plant was a weed and therefore somehow less. But nature doesn't know the word "weed." The trout lilies are no less beautiful for being hidden between rocks and sticks along the creek instead of planted neatly in the rows of a garden.

The questions run deeper than the sweet names of sprigs and the fragrance of a springtime blossom. They needle me at the leading edge of the person I am becoming.

I am listening now.

Beneath the gentle hushing of leaves ruffling in the breeze—the cluck of two branches arguing. They have grown so close that the wind shifts their weight and their barks rub and whine to the forest at their inseparability. There is the trickle of a spring that drips from the soft spongey filaments of winter-green moss. This isn't the sound of the land, you might argue, if you were in the mood to do such a thing. But, I would argue back, without land, the droplets of water would not dance so, would not dribble and plunk. Without land, the trees would never have rooted or had the strength to grow. The land's voice is the sound of existence brushing up against itself.

~

I love thunderstorms more than any other meteorological phenomenon. They are exactly the right blend of expected and unexpected. They are the only circumstance in which I willingly and joyfully let water soak me.

When I belly laugh, I sound like a cackling witch.

I love to make lists. I make them so I can see what I have done and what I have yet to do. I like the way they can organize a day or a week or a year. I enjoy immensely the feeling of crossing off items as they are completed. But know this, I will never cross off an item on a list that I did not personally complete. There is an honor system to lists. I follow it.

I rearrange the dishwasher when my husband fills it because I cannot help myself and because I firmly believe he does it wrong.

I have a strange affinity for benches. They are versatile, practical, and decorative. I find it extremely difficult to say no to a nice bench if I see one for a good price.

I have never broken a bone.

I believe there are certain things a person should never do. But I also believe that to grow into themselves fully, a person must do some of these things and learn to regret them.

Vandalism irks me.

I do not think I have a single secret. At least one other person on this earth knows my would-be secrets. If you are part of my life for long enough, and can be trusted, it is likely I will eventually share one with you. I don't like the idea of being one big mystery. I prefer to be a thousand small ones, traveling around the world within the people I love.

~

I hear the land now when I go walking in our woods and it is equally comforting and disquieting.

Disquieting: an odd word for a feeling brought on by the lack of human noise. How foolish for quiet to be disquieting. It is silent in the forest the way we are silent when our voices stop but our hearts loudly chatter on. A melody locked within itself, the vibration of living things living. What does the forest know of me as I move through it? Do the roots of these trees, their woody web carrying on in subterranean conversation, make note of my passing?

There is longing that flows between one's body and the forest air. An ache to be more than a witness to springtime's movement. To stand perfectly still in the sun as it sneaks between the leaves of an ash or an ironwood is to feel the fragility of each motionless moment in the light. Nothing lasts. Spring flowers are already falling to the oppressive heat. The air around me is salty sweet from my sweat evaporating into vapor.

We have no control of this movement from moment to moment. We cannot stay 23 or 39 or 50 forever. We have one year until we are moved without consent to the next. Until there are no more years and there are no more lily of the valley. This push is exactly what I need. You see, if time were to stand still and all of my movement through space relied on self-propulsion, I might find myself raking leaves into eternity. I cannot help it sometimes, busying myself with mundane tasks such as raking, shoveling, snipping unwanted brush. There is peace in the mindless. There is calm and quiet and space to relax into stagnation. I might fall into the quiet forever of one hand over the other, clearing trails on these 42 acres for my four children and our wild dog to run circles on.

Let me introduce myself: I am a woman who is connected to these 42 acres by a contract and it is unclear to me which party is responsible for the other. I am a mother of four young children. I am a wife. I am a person who is just now waking up into myself. I am a woman who thinks I have something to learn from this land, who is listening closely, hoping to understand myself just a little bit more.

The Orchard

I don't understand my husband's obsession with these trees.

From May through October, Nathan walks around with paint brushes covered in neem oil and sprayers primed to aerosolize organic pesticides and fungicides at the slightest hint of invasion. He's the fruit tree custodian around here and is remarkably diligent when it comes to keeping this orchard's trajectory toward production. He recently walked me to the underside of some lush branches to personally introduce me to the very first apple from the Baldwin tree. Then it was on to the dozen or so mulberries that were in an early stage of ripening. Last year we waited for the five mulberries to reach the perfect state of ripeness only to have our seven-year-old pick them, taste one, then leave the rest on the picnic table in the sun to shrivel and rot. It was a great loss that still strikes a sour note with Nathan, when mentioned.

One might think that the frigid winter months would give Nathan some respite from doing battle with those who would do harm to his beloved trees. Not so. These are the months in which he does his best strategizing. While bugs and fungus can be kept at bay with simple tactics, there is no foe more cunning than the deer. They are a constant threat and to stop them has proven a most complicated endeavor (i.e., it hasn't happened yet). In the spring, they love to nibble the tender new buds as they open to the heat. In fall, they'll steal the apples (if there are any) and if they're low enough to reach. In winter, they'll eat all the new growth from the year before because it is still soft and sweet and there isn't much else to scavenge for in the Maine woods.

One of my favorite tactics Nathan attempted was drilling holes through bars of soap to hang from our fruit tree branches to deter the deer. He employed me to seek out the most pungent and offensive bars that money could buy. I managed to procure a case of soap that carried such sickly sweet musk they'd throw your lungs into a spasm if inhaled too deeply. Drilling holes is satisfying on its own, but for some reason, drilling holes through this particular soap, one marketed as profoundly masculine to use it as a deer deterrent, spoke to my sense of the absurd. I'm not in the marketing game, but I like to imagine a commercial in which this soap is being sold as an attractant for female humans and a deterrent for forest creatures.

I digress.

Nathan is doing a tremendous job caring for these mulberry, apple, pear, and plum trees. He waters them, mulches them, and fertilizes them with nutrient mixes designed for maximum health and superior stamina against infestations. This year he was also thinking about companion planting some daffodils. It didn't happen, but he spent some time considering what that might look like.

Still, I don't understand his obsession with these trees.

I understand a lot of things about my husband. I understand that before nine in the morning, anything anyone says to him is almost immediately forgotten. I understand that he is not a multitasker. I have come to accept that he is not an individual who makes lists or keeps track of dates and appointments. But I do not understand how he can, week after week, remember to verify the leaves of his beloved trees are free from disease and plump with moisture. The very act of remembering a task like this is so out of character for Nathan that I can't help but approach his fastidiousness with suspicion.

Nathan barely remembers to put his clothes in the hamper. What is it about this orchard he is growing that has engaged his hippocampus?

~

Interesting fact: Nathan's heart only beats in the ballpark of 38 times a minute. I would be in a coma if my heart were beating that slowly. But his just hums right along like it's no big deal to hammer out half the average number of beats of a regular person every minute. And I do mean hammer. If you put your head to his sternum you don't just hear his heart, you feel it through his bones. The power of the thump is really quite something.

Nathan makes me laugh. You can't really overestimate how important that quality is in someone. When you're young and dating, people will say, "Do you make each other laugh?" And you think, yeah, sure, they're kind of funny sometimes and they seem to think I am too. But finding someone who makes you laugh isn't really about being funny. Nathan is himself and I get immense joy out of watching his life unfold next to mine. He can make me laugh when my heart is heavy. He can make me laugh when I'm exhausted and he wakes me up in the middle of the night with a ruckus. It's usually some catastrophe involving a child's toy that sings loudly, or an ill-placed stack of books that ends up under foot. But always, I'm glad I'm awake. He can make me laugh when the kids have us up at 4:30 in the morning on a Saturday and we're out of coffee. I find his idiosyncrasies endearing, his worldview baffling, and his choices always sound—he is a person whose very nature serves as a subconscious compass toward joy.

When Nathan holds our children, whether they are seven or seven months, he is whole. There is no part of him that he does not openly share. No compartment of his slow-hammering heart that does not flood with his love of being a father.

~

Recently, our Au Pair, Ally, gave Nathan and I some kid-free time over a long weekend. We were able to spend four hours working together in the woods clearing an old tractor trail down to the creek. Ruts from the ancient path are still there, following the hillside's curve, weaving through the gaps in the rock wall down through the valley. Nathan and I don't often get to spend time with one another without at least one or two of our children simultaneously making demands or threats, so this was a real treat. To leave the noise of our home and enter the cool forest on a spring day was blissful. It was also shockingly quiet, even with the melodic buzz of a chainsaw and the crashing of trees, their limbs snapping as they fell to the leaf-littered forest floor. Before having kids I'm not sure my definition of blissfully quiet would have included a chainsaw, but also before having kids I didn't know anything about the noise of a family like ours. We're a machine that rumbles and chirps in near constant protest to the motion of our own parts. As the kids grow and mature, I have no doubt the decibels will rise. Their voices will continue to demand to be heard. Our system, as imperfect as it is, is one that both Nathan and I appreciate for its nearly constant entropic decay and subsequent regrowth.

In the woods, Nathan and I were in our element. We worked together smoothly, without much need for words. During breaks, we drank water from a canteen and smiled at each other. We talked about our plans for the land, how this trail would hook to the one on the ridge, how the creek trail would cut toward us along the property boundary. Not many would consider brush clearing to be the perfect way to spend a morning with the person you love, but Nathan and I do. We are on the exact same page about our desire to use our land to the fullest. Forty-two acres is hard to understand until you've crisscrossed and zig-zagged through it, circumscribed it, and navigated it with a compass from corner to corner. Forty-two acres is a lot of land. But it is exactly the right amount of land for two people who sometimes need to escape the noise of raising four children. Who sometimes need to remember why they fell in love with each other and created a bunch of people who are constantly yelling at and threatening them.

~

And here's another thing. Nathan can be holding something in his hands and then (apparently) very deliberately do something with the item, like place it carefully in a drawer, and then have no memory of what happened to it.

Nathan can also play the piano beautifully. When he plays, and he thinks no one is listening, he puts all of himself into the music and it could take your breath away.

Something else I find fascinating is that he can see a person who he does not know doing something he does not understand and is completely detached from judgment about that person and what they are doing until he has more information. I have never seen anyone in my life so unwilling to make snap judgments about another human being. It's like they don't even occur to him. It's a beautiful thing to witness. I hope our kids learn to see people like he sees people. I can barely comprehend, I'm embarrassed to say, what it must be like to see others without doing so through the lens of my own psychological deficiencies.

~

Nathan suffers from color-blindness. Actually, no. Let me clarify that. I suffer from Nathan's colorblindness. He doesn't know any different, and to say he suffers might indicate I believe his ability to see is somehow less than mine, when in fact, it is merely different. It is I who suffers from his constant need to prove something when it comes to color. Prove what? I have no idea. I wish he would leave matters of color choice to me, but he won't. For someone who sees reds and greens in grayscale, he is rather opinionated about their practical application.

Sometimes I put my foot down about this or that, but when it's important, I have to consider his suggestions regarding color with the utmost seriousness. Such as the color of our house. Would I have decided in about thirty seconds what color of gray I wanted the shingles on our house? Yes. Absolutely. Did I do so? Yes. Absolutely. Did I also entertain a three-day-long charade in which Nathan and I each made two separate trips to a local hardware store to gather a truly mind-boggling number of samples of varying shades of gray? Yes, I also did that. I really do want Nathan to enjoy the shade of gray of our home when he drives up to it from a trip to the grocery store. But I also have a life to live and the hemming and hawing about minuscule shifts in color is a special kind of torture for me because I don't hem and haw about anything in my life. It's not in my nature. I make choices with terrifying speed. Often, they're decidedly not in the best interest of long-term success. Nathan knows this about me and so he takes it upon himself to be a loving roadblock in all things of import.

It might seem I'm trying to justify a tenuous relationship, but the simple truth is that I am, in my opinion, in the perfect marriage. Nathan is absolutely right to slow me down. Can you imagine painting your entire house and then deciding you hate the color? That's the kind of thing that would happen if I were let loose. Well, that's not exactly true. What would happen is that Nathan would hate the color of our house and I would convince myself retroactively that any color was actually fine because it was done and I did it and I'm not doing it again. I tend to justify poor decisions with these kinds of mental gymnastics, but Nathan's brain isn't so keen on fostering that kind of flexibility.

So, he makes me look at thirty different grays and we decide on a mix of four parts of Cottage Gray to one-part Cream in my Coffee and the hardware store employees are annoyed and I'm annoyed and Nathan is annoyed and the house looks great.

~

Confession: I broke the lawnmower for the twentieth time yesterday. I say twentieth, but in reality, I've probably done something that damaged the ol 'girl more times than that. It's not that I'm trying to be rough on her, but I never had a riding mower growing up, so getting to mow our expansive lawn on a riding machine is a chore I find extremely enjoyable. I get a little carried away and do things like mow into the forest. Just a little though. I'm not 500 yards deep into the underbrush or anything, but I do tend to wander from the conventionally accepted greenery into some more questionable areas. Last year I accidentally mowed an ax when I got too close to the woodpile. Yesterday, I think it must have been a stick from under the oak tree in the back field that got me. To my credit though, I do stop when I know something untoward has happened. I don't just keep on mowing like a lunatic.

Yesterday it was obvious something was wrong. It sounded like the mower was a jet getting ready to take off after the incident. I turned the blades off and drove the mower to the back of the house so that Nathan could have a look. There are few things my husband finds less pleasurable than small engine repair. There are few things I have broken quite so often as small engines. This is an unhappy coincidence for everyone. When notified of a problem, I can almost hear Nathan's bones creak as he shifts his weight up out of whatever chair he's sitting in. It's like the prospect of fixing a small engine ages him a couple of decades. I think it's a bit dramatic, but I usually try to hold my tongue because I don't know how to fix the mower and I really need to get back to mowing.

Nathan is a repairman who works best with company. It's the long hours locked in a dark garage alone, trying to diagnose a mechanical complication that really gets him down. I try to avoid putting him in this situation as much as possible. So, yesterday I stood with him and chatted amiably about how I was pretty sure the grass clippings that were blowing in the wind as I zipped around the property were heavy with brown tail moth caterpillar hairs and we were likely all doomed. These caterpillar hairs are currently everywhere because the caterpillars are everywhere and they are extremely toxic to humans. The rash that results from a run-in with one of these creatures is horrifically itchy and lasts for weeks. Right now in our county, the grocery stores are completely sold out of all anti-itch creams. I was in a store today picking up a few items and heard no less than four strangers talking to their shopping companions about their rashes.

Nathan discovered that the problem with the mower was not related to the engine and his relief was so great that he even chuckled. It was just a belt that came loose and he was able to pop it back on with a little of this and a little of that.

I was able to finish most of the mowing, but when I turned the mower off for a quick break around 4 p.m. to get some water, something else must have happened because at 4:15 p.m. when I tried to finish up the last little bit, the mower wouldn't start. I haven't had the heart to mention it again, but when Nathan finds the mower parked beside the house tomorrow instead of back in the barn, we're going to have to have an unpleasant conversation. To add insult to injury, I was right about the caterpillar hairs. I'm covered in a rash.

~

Nathan writes many of his letters like he's left-handed even though he is right-handed. I find his handwriting equal parts delightful and atrocious. He does not believe it so, but he is an incredible writer. I think, much better than I am. But when he writes, it is painful for him because he is, in this arena of his life, a perfectionist. A paragraph that I might write in two minutes will take him forty-five. His is better, but for him, it's not worth the cost.

At night, we read one book for each of our children before bed. But sometimes, when Nathan or I have the extra bit of energy needed to go one step further, we'll tell a story instead. Nathan tells the story of a five-year-old boy who lives with a rabbit and a phoenix in space. He calls the series "Space-Blaster Jack" and even though it was started when Jack was only 3 years old, all of the kids now know the stories and beg for them to be told and re-told. When Nathan makes up a Space-Blaster Jack story on the fly, I am always amazed by how smoothly the storyline flows, and how each character is developed and explored a little bit further. Everyone in our family cherishes these stories, myself included.

Nathan loves to play chess. If he is looking at his phone during the day, it is often because he is playing a match of speed chess with a stranger. He is delighted by how bad he is at speed chess because he is actively trying to improve. When Nathan is bad at something he is never upset. In fact, I sometimes wonder if he enjoys being bad at things more than being good at them because it means he is about to learn something new.

My husband loves to learn new things. I'm sure that sometimes he wishes the things he had to learn weren't related to small engine repair.

~

These forty-two acres that Nathan and I own, they feel big. But they are nowhere near as big as our commitment to our children, and to each other. Yet, somehow, the pull of the land has woven its way through each of us, wiggled and wedged itself deep into the gaps of this family to cement us to ourselves and to each other. We are inseparable, just now, neither party willing to release its hold on the other. Nathan has his trees. I have wild blueberries, lilac, and trillium. The kids have it all, the trees, the flowers, insects and snakes—and dark earth packed tight beneath their fingernails.

The Orchard

At lunchtime, without fail, Nathan invites me on a walk to the orchard. He invites the kids too, if they are near and show any interest at all. I used to think this habit was about his love for the trees—a way to bask in the successes of his careful tending. I'm a little ashamed to admit that I was annoyed at his near constant need to check up on them, inspect their bark for damage, ensure the soil at their base was well-watered. I would roll my eyes and only sometimes join him on these forays. But it has just now occurred to me that I have been looking at it the wrong way this whole time. Nathan is creating an orchard we can all enjoy together. He is, every day, working toward a future with this family on this land.

I understand it now, his obsession is not with these trees. Nathan is transforming his time into a living love, one that smells like apple blossoms in spring and tastes like the tangy juice of a mulberry.

Leeches

There is a juice jug on my front step filled to the brim with pond water. The jug doesn't have a lid because my 8-year-old son lost it when he was down at the pond. Instead, a board rests on top, presumably to prevent the creatures inside from attempting escape. In truth, the board is completely unnecessary because these are creatures that require water to live. To leave the bottle would mean certain death. I wish I were referring to pollywogs or tiny fish or even pond worms. I'm not. My son Jack has taken his love of fishing to a new and grotesque level—one where capturing his own bait becomes an integral part of the whole experience. The Internet informed him that leeches make good bait and now he's keeping hundreds of them alive in jugs all over the property. "Can't you dig for good old fashion worms?" I ask him. This statement falls into the category of questions I ask as a parent that I never thought I'd ask. It keeps good company—"Can you please stop rubbing cream cheese into your eyes," "Please don't eat rocks," "Please stop washing your hands in my drinking water and then not telling me you did it." Even though I should be used to making these disturbing requests, I find I am still surprised when one of them comes out of my mouth.

I'm not a fisherwoman so I do not know whether leeches are better than any other kind of live bait, but I do know that I like them a lot less than, say, every other invertebrate on the planet. My son would ask, "But why? They're just trying to live like any other creature." I don't have a great answer other than thinking I'm justified in my very natural evolutionary response to find animals that suck other animals' blood gross.

~

I have a friend who is nearing forty and has no desire to round her age in either direction. She is grappling with one of the biggest decisions of her life: deciding whether she wants to have children. I am fully aware that my opinions on the wonders of parenthood are not particularly useful to her and do my best to remain deeply committed to support her in her search for her own truth. That said, sometimes I share things with her that I realize only afterward might be unsettling to someone who is trying to parse their own feelings on the pros and cons of creating people. Truth is, someone who has kids is too close to the situation to give sound advice on whether someone else should do it. As is someone who has decided not to have kids. I like to imagine each of us having a private mathematical formula that either solves itself or lengthens infinitely as we move into our adulthood, searching for an answer. An equation that determines our ultimate decision to create people or something else. The act of creation seems inescapable—children, art, music, dance, poetry—we are made for it.

While I'd like to tell my friend that once you get the hang of parenting it gets easier, I can't. It never gets easier. It changes and sometimes it's changing so fast that there's no way to keep up. Don't get me wrong, there are many things that are completely intuitive about being a parent. You model certain behaviors and you're more likely to see those behaviors (not guaranteed mind you, just more likely) in your children. You treat your kids with respect, they are more likely to express themselves respectfully (after they pass through the ages of 0–5, before that, good luck on this front). But here's something unintuitive. If you do a good job at imparting certain skills, your life as a parent will become infinitely more difficult.

Example: You teach your kids to be suspicious of people spouting nonsense and give them the tools to develop an incredibly reliable B.S. meter and all of a sudden you need scientific articles to convince your offspring that you're not making something up on the spot to serve your own selfish purpose or sensibilities. (Which is often exactly what you're doing.) You teach your kid to be a free thinker and then boom, your every word is held under a microscope and examined for accuracy. You might as well get used to hearing "Hey Siri" every time you make a factual statement because Siri *will* be consulted. Your days of "Because I said so" are over. There is no turning back once a child has mastered these life skills.

~

This is the second summer in which Jack's fascination with leeches has served as a thorn in the side of our family. It started last year when Nathan and I made a truly appalling leech-related discovery. Discovery might be overstating it. Had it not been for Bellamy, who came running into the house to inform us that Jack was sitting on the patio with his prized "Papa Leech" digging in for a good meal on his forearm, we may never have known. While credit goes to Bellamy for shedding some light on the situation, it is unlikely her motivation had anything to do with safety or concern. She's not one to miss a good parental meltdown and her face was glowing with genuine delight as she explained how her big brother was playing host to a Papa parasite. She made sure to remain within earshot as we questioned Jack and energetically expressed our horror. Jack saw absolutely nothing wrong with his life choices, so he had no qualms about sharing his thought process. He was not only collecting leeches and keeping them in containers around the house, he was feeding them his own blood to sustain them (at least, the big ones he thought would make good bait). This made perfect sense to him because the small amount of blood it took to keep a leech going was peanuts to him, but would kill a smaller creature at the pond. Therefore, he was actually saving frogs' and fish's lives.

Sure, I know that bloodletting and leech therapy are things that exist. I am fine with this practice when other people choose to do it. But I draw the line at my then six-year-old son using his own blood to keep a bunch of gelatinous pond dwelling succubi alive. Nathan was even more aghast than I. He cautioned Jack that leeches carried disease and would surely give him some incurable ailment or life-threatening illness when they fed on him. To Jack's credit and to our eternal detriment, this child can sense when an adult is making something up on the spot. He looked Nathan straight in the eye and asked for proof from a scientist that he could get sick from a leech.

I'm no leech scientist, but I can use Google, and when I looked it up to try and help Nathan's argument, I was disappointed to discover that the general consensus is that leech bites do not make you sick. This line of argument was dead in the water and Nathan's credibility on the subject was instantly gone. Basking in the glory of having proven an adult wrong, Jack graciously agreed to stop feeding the leeches to pacify his father, not out of fear or disgust. I couldn't help but be impressed by the way Jack artfully twisted the act of doing what we wanted into a victory for him instead of one for us. It was almost as if what he was really saying when he agreed to stop serving his own bodily fluids to pond dwellers was, "I'm going to humor you on this one because it's not that important to me, but consider yourself warned, I will weaponize my social intelligence against you if necessary."

~

What I might share with my friend who is considering children of her own is how these small people that our bodies create quickly transform into beings that, in turn, begin to create. A child is a blossoming fractal. To watch a person grow is to be entangled by both gut-wrenching beauty and grief. It is to watch a sunrise knowing it will set before we have known the full warmth of the day. For me, becoming a parent has forced a reckoning. Life is as much about holding on as it is about letting go.

~

Despite the house rule prohibiting the feeding of leeches with human blood, Jack's interest in leeches does not appear to be waning. His collection began again this spring as soon as the water was warm enough to wade in. The jugs began to appear on front steps, back patios, and picnic tables. Jugs full to the brim with water and bustling with dozens of leeches.

At first, I assumed Jack was collecting these leeches with his hands or in a net when he was down at the town landing. As it turns out, the process through which these leeches are taken into custody is so much worse than that. My daughter Bellamy also goes down to the landing to play in the water. Stone skipping, doll swimming lessons, dinosaur fights, you name it, it happens at the landing. When I inquired as to how one procures such large quantities of leeches, I was informed that Bellamy has been serving as Jack's leech bait for over a year. He waits for her to attract the leeches as she plays in the water. He stands on a rock nearby and can see them coming. At least, the big ones. Sometimes the small ones attach to her without him noticing and he has to collect those when she gets out of the water by pulling them off of her feet and legs. But the big ones you can see slithering through the water when they catch her scent. These are his words. I have no idea whether leeches can catch a scent, and while I could ask Siri, I don't think I want to. I was incredulous the first time I heard this process explained. I immediately went to Bellamy to ask her if she 1) knew that she was Jack's leech attractant, and 2) was at all disturbed by this fact. Turns out, she was aware of the whole scheme and had her own reasons for accepting the terms. Apparently, she is going to play in the water regardless of whether her brother is perched close by, eagerly awaiting her attackers and she'd just as soon have him eliminating the big leeches before they find her. Her logic is solid, but I can't help wondering if I have gone wrong somewhere in my parenting.

This summer I have tried to impress upon Jack there is no point in bringing jugs of leeches home if he is not going to have time to use them all as bait. As much as I dislike finding jars of these things propped precariously on indoor and outdoor surfaces, I dislike more the idea that he is harming a living creature for no discernible purpose. This argument was one that hit home with him. I didn't need science to back up an ethical argument. Jack, unfazed by our distaste at his fascination with leeches, is not one to ignore a criticism regarding his treatment of a living creature. He does not want to hurt an animal, even a leech. So, he has agreed that no leech shall be kept for longer than a day. This is progress.

~

I've learned to savor moments of successful parenting, however small. In a day or a week or a year, sometimes that's all I have. These moments stack atop one another and my hope is that in the end, they're solid enough to support healthy, strong, opinionated, independent kids. The chaos and unquestionably insalubrious antics of these children are nothing my own mathematical formula could have predicted. But I do believe that, for me, the equation has always been in balance. When I go to bed after a long day of warning kids not to eat rocks and not to dig holes in the driveway and not to catch bees in Tupperware, I get no fewer than four goodnight hugs and four goodnight kisses to tip the scales back toward sanity. When I wake, tired from a sleepless night with a teething baby, I get no fewer than four good morning snuggles to help me start the day with joy.

As for the leeches, there has been one happy consequence to this whole situation. Whenever my kids see other kids or adults at the town landing or the swimming hole, they waste no time in explaining how prevalent the leeches are. It's the only time I appreciate their enthusiasm when it comes to these disgusting little bloodsuckers. Jack's animated descriptions of how large and numerous the leeches are have, I believe, helped to keep the outside traffic at our beautiful pond to a minimum. Sure, there are those willing to brave a dip in a leech-infested pond (my own family can be counted among them), but many will hop right back into their cars to find another more suitable spot to cool off.

Hatchets, Sword Fights, and Water Balloons

When people hear we have an Au Pair, the perception is that it is a fancy form of childcare. Maybe for rural Maine it is. But in truth, it is one of the most economical options for a big family with lots of children not yet in school. Not only that, it's an incredible opportunity for all of us to get to know someone from another country, who speaks another language, and who genuinely wants to be a part of our family. Our Au Pair, Ally, has been my savior from the moment she arrived from Venezuela almost two years ago. She is intelligent, kind, silly, and one of the hardest workers I've ever met. She makes four kids feel manageable when everyone knows that four kids are absolutely not manageable. You don't "manage" kids. They are wild creatures meant to explore, make mistakes, make messes, and in general give adults a hard time for being intractable and old.

~

There are a few Au Pair organizations in the US and they work with many other countries to help facilitate a one- to two-year stay in the US for young men and women looking to do a cultural exchange and earn a little money in the meantime. I first became aware this was an option through some targeted ad campaigns on social media. I must have been Googling: "How do I survive with so many kids?" or "Is being a mother supposed to turn your hair white?" because one of the social media platforms picked up on the fact that I needed some assistance. Au Pair ads started popping up and I was primed to pay attention.

We had a few Au Pairs before Ally. Our first Au Pair, Maria, was from Brazil. Her English was impeccable and she was bubbly and kind. Prior to her accepting the position with us, I tried to make it clear that there was not much of a social scene in Palermo, Maine. In hindsight, I should have probably said there was *no* social scene. I don't think someone can fully wrap their head around how remote we are until they are standing in a field and cannot see another house or hear a single city sound. Maria certainly hadn't fully understood. She was from a large city and in watching movies and sitcoms of American life had imagined that no matter where she found herself, she'd be walking to coffee shops and meeting vast numbers of likeminded 20-somethings, including a wide range of available suitors. In Palermo, Maine, she met leeches, porcupines, and the occasional skunk.

It also didn't take long to figure out that Maria didn't particularly like kids. She wasn't mean to them, but she didn't enjoy games, sporting activities, swimming, or outdoor merriment of any kind. This was a problem that felt fairly difficult to overcome, as she was tasked with caring for our young children for almost 40 hours a week. We tried to work it out for a few months, but when she started making up completely baseless rules to make her job easier, things started to unravel.

Jack was just six at the time of Maria's arrival. If you have never dealt with a six-year-old child, you might not be aware that at six, most kids don't care for boundaries. When someone starts creating extra boundaries that don't make any sense, daily life becomes a battle. We have raised all of our kids to question authority. If a grown-up tells them to do something stupid, we'd like them to be able to distinguish that from reasonable requests and make a smart decision. Maria began to systematically destroy the kids' ability to do this.

Jack often ran to Nathan and me for confirmation that a new rule was completely outrageous. At first, we tried to simultaneously not undermine Maria while validating Jack's worldview. We explained to Jack that in other cultures, kids have different limits and adults have different comfort levels with what children can reasonably do unsupervised. We would have to tell and show Maria how things worked in our family and give her a chance to get familiar with us. In our family, six-year-olds can use hatchets if they follow our safety standards. In other countries (and families in our own country), this might be considered ludicrous. We tried convincing Jack that some of these misunderstandings were perhaps a result of cultural and familial differences. But when rules like: "Kids can't use markers before lunch" and "Jack can't play with sticks" started cropping up, we had to acknowledge what was really going on.

Bellamy and Ogden were too small to know what was happening, but Jack was a miniature lawyer. He needed evidence, proof of parental buy-in, and a logical reason for any request. Maria usually didn't have any of these things. She was agitated by Jack's finely calibrated BS meter and despite his ability to identify when she was creating boundaries to minimize her workload, she continued to do it.

Maria was horrified by most of Jack's hobbies, including but not limited to: catching snakes, digging for worms, playing with leeches, creating bug habitats, and caring for ant colonies. In response, she unilaterally decided the kids couldn't go outside for the first three to six hours of the day (depending on her mood).

Quite understandably, Jack ignored her.

Maria said kids weren't allowed in the upper field because it was a long walk and she didn't want to carry a baby up a hill to check on them.

Jack ignored her.

Jack and Maria were in near constant conflict during the day. She would make up a rule that didn't make sense to him. He would ignore it. She would get mad and make up more rules. As a result, Jack's brain was slowly being programed to ignore all information his caregivers gave him. That mentality started to bleed into his interactions with Nathan and me.

Maria had to go.

She agreed, and I think felt some relief that with a new family she might be able to find a situation where the children weren't so young, feral, and confrontational and the coffee shops weren't so distant. We parted amiably.

When Maria left, our whole family had to spend time finding its center again. Nathan and I had to remind Jack that not all rules were nonsensical. We had to restore his faith in adults.

~

Aside from Maria and Ally, we have had one other Au Pair. She was from Turkey and our children fondly remember her. Damla was also a lovely human. I can, in hindsight, remember her quite fondly too. But in all honesty, I do not believe I have lived a more stressful three months in all my life as during the time she lived with us.

Damla came from a family where small children were prized above all else. She absolutely loved the kids. She wanted to hug and kiss them non-stop, which might have been the only thing about her that our kids didn't like. She explained to us that in Turkey, small kids were treated like kings and queens and given whatever they wanted. To her discredit, she explained this in front of our kids. Jack wasted no time in capitalizing on this new and exciting information. When Nathan and I were working, he began to make requests that would have received an immediate "no" from the other adults in his life.

"Can we use Mama's blown glass fancy cups for a tea party in the forest?"

"Sure!"

"Can we throw all of the stuffed animals in the kiddie pool in the back yard and cover them in dirt?"

"Why not?"

"Can we spread play dough all over the windows and call it art?"

"Absolutely!"

"Can we have Oreo cookies for lunch?"

"We really shouldn't."

"Please?"

"Oh alright!"

The house devolved into complete chaos in a matter of days. The kids were malnourished, the floors were covered in debris, the walls in paint smears and marker lines. I was too afraid to go into my office for more than a few minutes at a time. As a technical writer and quality assurance associate for a pharmaceutical company, it was paramount I stay focused on my work, yet also absolutely impossible to do so. I couldn't leave Damla alone with the kids for more than ten minutes before some catastrophe arose. There was a fairly significant language barrier, so after requesting any given change in behavior and receiving a confirmation that it was understood, the same behavior would continue. To this day I am uncertain of whether Damla really knew what I was talking about. Ever.

She was so kind and loving that we really tried to work through some of these kinks with communication and direction.

It was during Damla's stay that Jack experienced his crowning achievement as a miscreant. He loves to tell the story of how it unfolded and how he knew all along that it was complete insanity. While I was out grocery shopping, he convinced Damla that it would be O.K. to hang water balloons from the living room ceiling on strings. He cajoled her into agreeing that it was only water and could be mopped up easily. At first, his plan had been to create an obstacle course the kids could run through, trying *not* to pop the balloons. But when that game got boring, he came up with something better and ran out of the house looking for the wiffleball bat. At this point, as he tells it, Damla looked a little nervous. He roped Bellamy into his new game so that the punishment, if it came, would be shared. Then, the two of them took turns swinging at balloons, hoping they would explode. Which, they did.

I arrived on the scene just after the third balloon had burst and water was dripping down three of the four walls, pooling in cracks between floorboards, soaking the rug and couch cushions. When he saw my face, Jack ran out of the house faster than I'd ever seen him run.

Damla's stay with us was one mess after the other and for me, instead of the workload being divided it was multiplied (by a factor of 10). Even so, Damla stayed. It wasn't until the really impossible complication arose that we had to help her find another family. We live so rurally that our Au Pairs have to know how to drive. We provide them a vehicle to borrow when they want to go find friends who aren't quilled.

Damla had informed us that she was comfortable behind the wheel and that she had a license in Turkey. It was winter when she arrived though, and she wasn't comfortable practicing in snow right away. She wanted to make sure her language skills had improved a little so she could get lessons on road rules while she practiced driving. About a month and a half after arriving, Damla took her first practice drive with Nathan. They both nearly died. Many times. She drove through the ditch leaving the driveway. She took her first sharp turn at 60 mph. She almost rolled the car taking her first intersection at high speed.

Nathan was visibly shaken when they returned. All he could mutter at first was, "I think we have a problem." When he'd had a few minutes of sitting on the couch quietly he informed me that he didn't believe that Damla had ever driven a *car* before. She had learned on a tractor.

Damla was disappointed that we asked her to leave, but she understood our reasons. We didn't have the time to spend 120 hours of practice driving time to get her license in Maine, nor were we convinced that 120 hours would be enough. We also didn't have the time or energy to watch her watching our kids.

~

Then we found Ally. She has two younger brothers and had been caring for a cousin in Venezuela for almost a year. She was well versed in the behavior of kids. Her English was good, but had room for improvement, and she loved to play. She also almost immediately began to correctly intuit when to say yes and when to say no in line with our family's values.

No to water balloons in the house.

Yes to kids climbing trees as high as they felt comfortable.

No to sword fights with shovels.

Yes to painting your whole body with watercolors if you promised to jump in the bath when you were done.

Ally knew how to have fun with the kids but wasn't afraid to set a boundary that protected a life, prevented property damage, or caused disproportionate work for the adult who had to clean it up.

I have loved Ally from the very beginning. The kids have too. She makes every day easier by helping out with laundry, dishes, cleaning kid messes, and keeping the house tidy in general. But more than the chores she does, her presence here makes our family feel complete. When she leaves for a vacation, the kids ask when she will be back. They want to call her to see her face. They want to tell her about their day. I have not yet prepared myself for when Ally has to leave our family to go out on her own. She has become like a daughter to me, someone I am deeply protective and proud of.

Ally makes so much of our lifestyle here in rural Maine possible. Not only that, she seems to genuinely enjoy that lifestyle with us.

During the summer, almost every morning, the kids yell for Ally to help them get ready to go to the town landing or the swimming hole at the pond. I can hear them from my office.

"Ally, can you please help me find my bathing suit?"

"Of course! Let's go get it."

"Ally, can you please help me find my tackle box and fishing pole?"

"Of course! I think it's in the barn. I'll go with you."

"Ally! Where is my leech container from yesterday?"

"Near the coffee pot."

"Ally, can you pack us some snacks?"

"Yes. If you can tell me two words in Spanish."

"Leche. Serpiente."

"Good. What snacks do you want today?"

Ally is always there to help. She has superhuman energy reserves and is exactly the big sister these kids need.

When Bellamy wants to print pictures from her favorite cartoon to practice coloring, or when she wants to protect her paper dolls with contact paper, Ally is ready with supplies. When Ogden wants to crash cars on the kitchen floor or play Go Fish, Ally is on the floor with him, laughing, crashing, playing. She is walking patiently behind Ezra as he toddles up and down the hillside, enjoying the simple act of walking.

Right now, as I write, I can see Ally outside the living room window. She is carrying a twenty-pound paving stone from one spot to another in the yard so that Jack can make a queen ant trap. At least, that's my guess. I'm not sure why else she'd be doing it. Even though I can almost guarantee that Jack is building this ant trap where he shouldn't be, I can't help but smile that he and Ally are doing it together. She enables these kids to explore the world, without judgment.

She sets limits and has rules that make sense for the kids, but there is no boundary—no outer limit to her love for them.

It also doesn't hurt that she's a fantastic driver.

Today on the Farm: Dada

I have been asking Ezra to say "Mama" for the last six months.

The moment he began making intentional noise, I was there, in his face, moving my lips with deliberate care in the shape of "Mmmmm."

I changed his diapers and said, "Mama."

I nursed him and said, "Mama."

I fed him his first solid foods and while he chewed with his toothless mouth, I said. "Mama."

Naturally, Ezra's first word was, "Dada."

This did not deter me. I was happy for Nathan, who has never had a child say his name before mine. Though, I should be clear that in this house, Nathan is "Papa" so technically Ezra's first word was a generic reference to men who are fathers in other houses. I suppose splitting hairs doesn't serve anyone. Point is, it was fine. I was delighted Ezra was making any noises at all. No need to be picky.

But things have ratcheted up a bit, in my opinion. As a one-year-old, Ezra is absolutely aware that I am Mama. If asked, "Where is Mama?" he will point at me. This, while extremely encouraging, is also the source of my frustration. When I sit in front of Ezra and I ask him to say "Mama," he looks me straight in the eye and says, "Dada."

Intentional word choice.

Let me be clear, I have heard Ezra say, "Mama" before. He said it to Tulip (a dog!). He said it to a chair. He said it to a marker. There is no mistaking the fact that he knows how to say it. It is also my firmly held belief that he knows how badly

Today on the Farm: Dada

I would like him to say it. Therefore, I am left to conclude that he has been gifted with an extremely elevated sense of humor.

As a person who has done a little research into the nature of humor, I find it impressive and disconcerting that Ezra appears to be operating within the construct of the benign violation theory of humor. The premise being that in order to be funny, something must in some way be benign or harmless yet also have some facet that is a violation of either social norms, expectations, or cultural standards.

Ezra is a baby and babies are harmless.

I think the violation is obvious. Such cold-hearted, deadpan humor just isn't appropriate for someone in a size 3 diaper.

Body and Soil

I walk barefoot most of the year. The soles of my feet are thick, calluses built upon calluses. I can walk across a gravel driveway as though it were smooth tile, bear the crags of rock beaches and the chunks of cement littering our front yard, which right now is a construction zone. It brings me great pleasure to report the kids are the same. Like mine, their feet are rarely confined to the inconvenient pressure of a shoe or slipper. You see, I am a firm believer in the communion between foot and earth. I am not a religious person, but I do believe in holy things.

It can be delicate, even within the confines of one's own head, to approach thoughts of holiness. What we recognize as sacred, even to ourselves, gives voice to vulnerabilities, puts into the world our deepest need to assign meaning. These things are holy to me: The cool fluffy soil of a freshly tilled field. The dew slick grass on a cool spring morning. The slimy mud surrounding the base of pickerel weed plants at the edge of the pond.

No.

That isn't quite right. Holy is the moment my feet touch these places, the connection between a body and its place on this planet, in this solar system, in this universe. Sacred are the neurons firing from the base of my body to the top, telling me the grass tickles as it touches the space between toes.

When things become chaotic, we are told to stay grounded. It seems to me there is a fundamental recognition of the power of the earth's touch.

~

In another lifetime, I worked as a sales representative in a large mall for a company that made cloyingly sweet lotions and perfumes. I didn't much like the work, but it paid a decent hourly wage and allowed me to live and work in a new city. It also placed me in direct contact with an odd breed of human. The kiosk worker. These salespeople were involved in a wide variety of marketing schemes. There were custom-made signs, fancy slippers, sunglasses, customized jewelry and even spa workers offering oddly personal services such as facials and body massages in the center of a busy shopping mall.

I find the idea of hawking most of these items distasteful, but in particular, one practice stuck with me for the last twenty years as mind bogglingly strange. The ionic detoxifying foot bath. This is a practice of soaking one's feet in some water with a couple of electrodes to "remove toxins from the liver" or "change the body's pH" or "pull toxins from the blood through your feet." Some people believe in this therapy. I am not one of them. While I do not profess to be an expert on any method of healing, traditional or otherwise, I do have a degree in the biological sciences. This detoxification method does not pass my sniff test. That said, I appreciate it is a practice that recognizes (one might say preys on the belief) that our feet are a conduit to better health.

~

Before having children, I was completely disgusted by feet. The idea of touching someone else's foot was horrifying. Smelling someone else's foot, out of the question. Babies changed this for me. Babies have feet so soft and pure that you'd be insane not to want to hold them in your hands, rub them against your cheeks. To breathe in the scent of a baby foot is to smell dreams as they twist and turn through the heart of the universe. What I mean is that it is incomparable. Before a child learns to walk, their feet are a thing untouched by this world, they are magic. There is a reason adults all over the world play with the sweet toes of their infants. "This Little Piggy" is an excuse, a fairly ridiculous one, to touch the toes of a baby, even one belonging to a stranger.

~

These 42 acres are legally ours. Well, technically, they are legally mine and also belong to someone who shares my husband's first and last name, but has a different middle initial. I enjoy holding this paperwork error over Nathan. Should another Nathan with the legal middle initial of "F" appear on the scene, I'll have to take a close look at his credentials and determine which of the Nathans I want to share this home with. Until then, Nathan S. and I share responsibility for the mortgage and the care of this place as though we were both legally bound.

I digress. What I was going to write was this: These 42 acres are legally ours, but the land isn't ours. We are merely squatters for a time. Maybe our kids will stay here after we're gone, but probably not. Jack imagines himself living in a futuristic sky city and if given the chance, I'm fairly certain Nathan would have himself launched into space to try colonizing whatever planet or asteroid happened to be available. Bellamy exists in an ephemeral world of words, her imagination drifts like a feather in the breeze. Ogden and Ezra have yet to express their intent to float away, but I feel it must be imminent. I deeply appreciate these extraordinary people and their exploratory spirits, but I am also concerned that not one of them imagines themselves with their feet on the ground.

I must use this time wisely. The time we live here. We have the privilege of feeling these 42 acres beneath our feet. It is my job to walk barefoot with these children into the blueberry barrens, to teach them to pick their way between the sharp sticks. I will explain how stepping too lightly can cause needless pain, the sharp edges of dry grass blades cutting and poking. I must show them how to step without fear and with the full weight of their bodies to transform a path into one that yields.

~

"Groundology" or "Earthing" are right up there with ionic detox foot baths for me. These are terms for the idea that to have one's feet in direct contact with the earth provides specific health benefits related to transferring electric impulses and electromagnetic communication between the body and the earth. Sniff test says bologna. But again, I think there is a seed of truth hidden at the core of these wonky pseudo-scientific money-making ploys.

People seem happier when they're touching the soil. Why this idea surprises people or gives them ideas of electromagnetic corrections to human physiology confuses me. Of course people are happier when they're touching soil. Usually when we're barefoot we're also doing something relaxing. We're at the beach, we're on a walk through a park, we're playing with our kids in the backyard. Our brains are letting go of meetings and to-do lists and every other manner of stress. When we're in nature, nature pulls us from ourselves.

We are the crafters of our own stress responses. We take ourselves from the quiet and submerge our brains in a constant barrage of input. We are always doing—rarely resting.

~

This past winter, snuggled beneath the cozy covers, my littlest baby did as each of his siblings before him. Even in sleep, his warm feet found the cool skin at my middle. They kneaded and pushed, toes curling and poking at the softness of a belly stretched from carrying them. His feet seemingly frantic, sought a place of grounding, of connection. As the seasons changed, there were too many shifts to track, but this one was not lost on me: By summer Ezra had learned to feel the soil beneath his feet. It was his first summer of walking and though I am happy to have a child with the ability to move himself, there was a great loss that also happened. The impossibly smooth skin of his feet's arches, the delicate pink of his heels and the pads of his toes have faded. He now walks upon heels and toes caked with dirt. Tiny muddy footprints appear on the kitchen floor when he comes in for a snack. His perfect feet no longer seek my belly for connection, they reach and pull and scream for the ground. The earth is calling this child, asking to take the place of what came before.

~

I ran into an old acquaintance at the grocery store today. I had to circle around the cheese and bread-roll aisle two or three times to convince myself it was really him because as far as I knew, he was living in Finland. I did what any sane person does when they can't figure out if a stranger is someone's doppelganger or the real deal. I yelled his name. Sure enough, he was visiting for a short while, packing up his life into a three-foot by five-foot box to send to Finland upon the sale of his old farmhouse.

We chatted amiably for a few minutes. This man was the father of a good friend of mine growing up and while I would not consider him in any way close to me, he is a part of my history, and dear to me in the way that pieces of ourselves are dear as they fade into memory. On the way home I was struck by how uncomfortable I was imagining myself making the choice that he was making. He and his wife had raised three kids in rural Maine. They had land and, in my mind, had always been connected to their gardens and fields and woodlots.

But here they were, selling all of it. People call this "uprooting" a life, but is that really accurate, metaphorically? It doesn't feel like they are pulling roots from the ground, it feels to me like they are leaving them behind. I am heartbroken but am having trouble pinpointing for whom. Maybe it is a personal failing, to be too connected to a particular place on this planet, unwilling to imagine that roots are not physical, but metaphysical. To assume that without this land or that land it will be impossible to connect ourselves to nature, our pasts, our roots.

~

And then there is reflexology, defined by the American Reflexology Certification Board as, "a non-invasive, complementary practice involving thumb and finger techniques to apply alternating pressure to reflexes shown on reflex maps of the body located on the feet, hands and outer ears." Pressure to a toe targets the pineal gland, pressure to an arch for the gall bladder. What I think about this therapy is irrelevant (but probably obvious, at this point). But I don't mention it to discredit it. I am fascinated by its existence. By the existence of all of these ways in which people have targeted the feet to work toward overall health.

The body is a highly evolved biological machine. Is it possible to believe that alternating pressure to your feet might improve your health? Of course it is. Do I believe that improvement is due to the targeted pressure on your big toe? No.

And yes.

I am rather relaxed when I get a foot rub. Relaxation, physical contact, belief that one is being helped (placebo effect), all of these things trigger a cascade of hormones and chemical responses in our bodies. Could some of those responses make you healthier? Absolutely.

Despite not really knowing the answers to what makes us feel good, humans continue to use their intuition about feet to create pathways toward health.

~

I admit, the earthing fad strikes an almost spiritual chord within me. While the scientific claims are laughable, I can't help feeling that for me, there is something deeper at play. I am, in a sense, an "Earther." Holiness cannot be scientifically quantified. What is sacred to me does not require proving in a scientific journal. It need only satisfy my personal qualifications. It need only bring me closer to an understanding of myself. For me, the earth's touch is indeed a conduit to health.

Some might argue it isn't the earth touching us at all, but the other way around. But I'm not so sure who should be credited with the intent of this connection. Which party initiated this relationship between body and soil? I may walk upon the ground, but without the earth to grow my food, without the soil to sprout trees and flowers and greenery that pull carbon dioxide from the air and replace it with oxygen, I wouldn't be here at all.

I imagine myself a beetle moving this way and that as the earth shuffles her hands and fingers to support the erratic scuttling of a creature, she has lifted from the cosmos to more closely examine it. I will eventually take flight or be put down into the infinite elsewhere.

For now, I'm just trying to keep my feet on the ground.

Machinery

When Nathan was in high school, he took an aptitude test that revealed he was best suited for a job running heavy machinery. There are times when the movement of this family through the world feels mechanical—carseats, laundry, mealtime, grocery shopping, sports, school. There are procedures, rules, steps to follow. But then, there is this:

Nathan and Bellamy are sitting on the couch together with a beginner book, level A. This is the first level of book for kids who can figure out words based on letter sounds. Nathan asks, "What does this funny-looking letter sound like?"

Bellamy laughs, "It's not funny looking. That's just an 'm,' Papa. It sounds like mmmm." They go on this way, with Nathan making a joke about the shape of a letter and Bellamy correcting him, or laughing at his ignorance, while sounding out the word "mat" and then "cat" and then "dig."

I watch while trying to make it seem like I'm not watching. Bellamy doesn't like being vulnerable like this. Not knowing is hard for her. But with Nathan, she giggles easily, sure that she is the one giving instruction. Nathan tells her he is getting tired, that he thinks she must be tired too. He says he doesn't want to do too much, hurt her brain. This makes Bellamy roll her eyes and work harder still. She hasn't yet run out of steam.

~

Nathan holds Ogden's hand as they step onto the wheel of the rusted yellow tractor in the garage. The tractor isn't running, it hasn't for months. But from atop the wheel, they can see three baby birds snuggled up in a nest. "What are they doing Papa?" he asks.

"They're opening their mouths to ask for food. They think we might be their Mama or Papa."

This makes Ogden laugh. "I'm not a bird!"

"You're not?" Nathan asks. He probes Ogden's armpits for feathers, sniffs his neck to determine which species this small creature is, if not a bird. This makes them both laugh, and Ogden's arms wrap tightly around Nathan's neck as they both come back down to the ground.

~

Nathan asks Jack if he wants to go for a quick jog. "Yes!" Jack screams as he races up the stairs to get his shorts and socks. The two of them disappear down the road at a pace I know I couldn't keep. They have the same physique, long muscular legs, almost no body fat. They know each other well enough to keep moving when they are together. For them, the conversion of food to fuel, the tightening of muscle fibers in anticipation of the next long stride, and the motion of their bodies is a language all its own. They connect best at high speeds because Jack is always at high speed and is often irritated by people who slow him down.

~

Nathan is singing quietly to Ezra, who is dosing on his chest. They are laying on the couch in the living room and even though the other kids are buzzing around them, crashing matchbox cars and roaring with dinosaurs in hand, Ezra is breathing slow and deep. I wonder if somewhere in his subconscious he remembers Nathan's voice as it sang to him in the NICU.

When Ezra was born, he had to be flown to Eastern Maine Medical Center and placed on a cooling table. The doctors kept his body at 93 degrees for seventy-two hours, hoping to prevent damage to his brain, which had been deprived of oxygen for over five minutes. Nathan stayed by his bedside, watched the EEG for changes when his voice talked softly, when he sang, when he played messages from Mama on the phone.

The hospital room hummed and whirred, every alarm a curiosity or concern, every beep and click a step closer to taking our baby home.

~

Nathan has yet to feel the rush of adrenaline while ripping tree stumps from the ground with an excavator bucket. He has never transported two-ton rocks from one place to another with a bulldozer, or swung the boom of a giant digger. But I think he's found the work for him. Fatherhood is sometimes about the moving parts of a family. Most of the time, it is about little moments, letter sounds and tiny birds, a racing heartbeat, or a slow and steady one lulling the baby to sleep.

Woodpile

Making most woodpiles goes something like this: A tree is cut down. The tree is limbed (meaning the small useless branches are removed), then the remaining logs are cut into rounds that are either split immediately or stacked for later splitting. When eventually split into firewood, the wood is stacked neatly in any number of ways. I say, "any number of ways," but in my opinion, there is one best way, which is as a giant rounded pile that sheds water naturally while the wood dries. And it should be dry. Wet wood burns more slowly (or not at all) and can be the cause of a creosote build-up inside the chimney. I digress. The wood is stacked and then the wood is used all through the winter until the pile has disappeared and the cycle starts over.

Anyone who knows the aforementioned cycle also knows that I've simplified a few things, and that the cycle is always in motion because if you don't have wood drying while you're using wood, you'll end up with no dry wood next winter, so there are no breaks. But this detail is neither here nor there in the story I am about to tell.

We have one woodpile on our property with a long and not so proud history. In my mind, it has become a blazing torch of a reminder that this family is completely uninterested and perhaps incapable of learning the very basic New England skill of doing it right the first time.

Upon moving to our farmland four years ago, we realized we were going to need some wood to burn in the kitchen's potbellied stove to get us through the winter. This was a romantic notion indeed. A cozy kitchen with our two, soon to be three children sitting lazily on the kitchen floor playing card games or making up stories with toy dinosaurs while basking in the warmth. If you have kids, you've already identified several gaping holes in this fantasy. Kids don't play quietly anywhere. They certainly don't bask. In addition, it should be noted that having small kids near a wood stove is a constant source of anxiety. Even so, we ordered the firewood because regardless of whether it was going to be romantic, we needed the pipes to refrain from freezing solid.

Three cord of wood was delivered. A fairly large dump truck drove across the yard and around the house to deposit the "split," "dry" wood. It was neither. Nathan and I had to go out there with our axes and chop about half of the pieces into two or three smaller pieces because they wouldn't fit into the stove. After getting them all to size, we moved this wood into our dilapidated woodshed, which at that time, was attached to the house and in danger of collapse.

In the narrative of a normal woodpile, the wood is getting fairly close to returning to the atmosphere, passing to the next phase in the carbon cycle. Not our wood. Things were just heating up.

The first winter, we realized the wood was so wet it wouldn't burn. It sat in our woodshed and we decided to buy another cord of wood from a man who had a picture of his woodpile on Uncle Henry's, a Maine staple for anyone looking to buy, sell, or offload items for free. The man said his wood was dry and in the picture, he had a long stack of wood against a house. For those not familiar with how much wood is in a cord, imagine this: a cord of wood is a neatly stacked pile of rounds that measures four feet tall, by four feet wide, by eight feet long. We were looking to buy split wood that was cut to about 16 inches in length, so the pack was expected to be slightly tighter, but for the purpose of this explanation, the reader can assume, we knew what a cord of wood would look like because my father has explained it to me about 80 times and I have moved and split many dozens of cord of wood in my lifetime.

What became immediately clear from an extremely confusing back and forth with the man selling his wood was that he did not know what a cord of wood looked like. The haggling over how much wood he had and his price lasted several days and prior to its completion, the man loaded the wood into his truck and drove it to our house. I think it can be universally agreed upon that having items delivered to your house before you agree to buy them is bad business. I will say, my memory has conveniently removed the part of this story where the man gets my home address before I have agreed to a price. Mistakes were made.

In the end, thank goodness, the extra almost-half-cord of wood we got for an almost-good price was dry. It burned great and we made it through the winter with little fuss.

But let's get back to that wet pile of wood.

The second winter in our farmhouse, the original three cord had dried down significantly. We began burning the wood as the nights grew cold. September passed without incident, then October, but as we moved our way deeper into the pile, strange things began to happen. Chicken feathers appeared between the rows. We did not have chickens. Pieces of garbage and compost items were discovered almost daily as we loaded up our arms to bring the wood into the kitchen. I became less interested in going to the woodpile and more interested in turning the thermostat to the oil burner in the basement a little higher. Under the ruse of protecting the purity of our air for the small children breathing it, I suggested we switch to oil when possible. This tactic was accepted with no argument and the second winter passed with sporadic fires all started and fed by Nathan, who did not seem to notice that rats were clearly running the show in that woodshed.

Year three is where the real foolishness began. In year three, after moving to this property, we decided it was time to get rid of the old woodshed so we could either build something smaller and simpler, or put an addition on our house. Regardless of the path, we needed to tear down the old structure. That meant the wood needed to move. For about three days, Nathan and I made trips from the dank recesses of that woodshed, braving rat feces, chicken bones from kills long before our time, and the smell of garbage to transport armfuls of wood to a new stack, just outside the back door. This was now the second time we were carting around at least two cord of wood. The wood sat outside our back door all fall, a tarp was draped over it and the woodshed was torn down.

That winter, for some reason, we burned almost no wood. We had a baby in the house and were both working long hours and found ourselves relying much more heavily on the oil-burning furnace. Then, as summer rolled around, we realized it was unsightly to have a giant pile of wood right next to the back door, plus I was thinking of building a patio, so I needed the space to be able to dig and clear. The woodpile was moved a third time, to the side of the house.

Things get a little fuzzy at this point. Maybe what I mean to say is, things get a little embarrassing. I built the patio, so the third transport of this wood seemed worth it in the end. But then winter rolled around again and the wood on the side of the house was just too far away to make sense. It was moved back to the grass next to the new patio.

Move four.

During that fourth winter we burned about half the wood. And the pile, significantly smaller, didn't seem as difficult to move back to the side of the house to keep the back yard clear for summer fun.

Five.

But then we decided to sand blast the old shingles on the house to remove the hideous red paint and the woodpile on the side of the house was in the way, so Nathan's father helped us chuck the pile about four feet to the left so that we had room to put the ladders and the blaster equipment.

Six.

And then, the pile was blocking the route from the front yard to the back yard and construction had started on the addition, so it needed to be clear for the workers' vehicles and for our mower. The wood was carried back to a stack outside the back door.

Seven.

Seven is my lucky number because it is my last name spelled backward. I like to think we've reached the end of this charade, but I honestly don't know where this family is headed and there is still at least three quarters of a cord stacked outside our back door right now. Truth be told, the patio isn't really working out. We've thought about putting in a deck, but the woodpile is in the way.

Today on the Farm: Day Eight

Today is day eight. Eight days without Ally to help me run this house. She is on vacation and without her, things have been hectic and messy. Nathan is in his home office for most waking hours, while I am homeschooling the older kids, trying to work part time as a technical writer, feed everyone, keep the laundry from overtaking us, prevent Ezra from putting everything in his mouth, and attempting to keep enough of our dishes clean at any given time to allow for hygienic mealtimes. I am experiencing moderate to severe failure in every single arena of mothering and life.

Eight days without Ally makes me wonder if we're crazy for trying to raise four kids. I know people raise more than four and do it splendidly. It's possible to have 8, 10, 12 kids. If Jack were reading this, he would tell me, "It's possible to have 69 kids, Mama." He read that in the *Guinness Book of World Records* last year and has not ceased being impressed by it. I can't even begin to fathom having 5 kids, let alone 69.

I have many friends who have chosen not to have kids. They are supportive and loving of my choice to do so, but are also a wonderful source of validation when it comes to the exhaustion I feel as a parent. It is so lovely to have someone look at your life and say, "Watching you makes me tired." For some reason, this simple acknowledgement that my life *looks* exhausting is comforting. If what I were doing didn't look hard, I might wonder if I were somehow doing it wrong. Is it supposed to be invigorating to make four breakfasts, lunches, and dinners, to brush four sets of teeth twice a day, wash endless laundry and try to keep the kids and their environment clean? These tasks feel absolutely draining. Raising kids is hard.

Raising kids is also so full of joy that the hard moments, most of them, feel completely worth it.

Today, Ezra said, "Mama."

Today, Oggie asked if I would keep him in my heart if I went to the grocery store without him.

Today, Bellamy held my hand when we walked outside to get the mail.

Today, Jack and I laughed hard at a joke we both thought was funny.

It was a good day.

Snow Day

Today was a snow day. A Nor'Easter blew in last night and the snow was whipping about the windows, teasing, daring the kids to come out to play. They ate a hasty breakfast and by 7:15 as the sun was beginning to lighten the blustery sky, the decision was made. Not by me. The kids have learned to make their own decisions before coffee has been consumed. They're usually poor and require inordinate adult supervision or involvement, but at least I don't have to make them.

Finding the gear is the first step. But as I search for lost boots and mittens, I notice all three kids are in a state of undress. It seems obvious to me that one requires underwear to go out into the snow, but I appear to be in the minority. The kids are instructed to find underwear, socks, pants. This, I hope, is going to buy me some time to drink coffee in peace, but of course the stairwell is too dark and full of monsters so I must follow them to their individual dressers while holding the baby and clarifying that a bathing suit is indeed NOT underwear, and a tutu is not pants. This goes on for a period of time that feels endless but probably lasts no more than two minutes.

If you have children under the age of ten, or have cared for such children, you will be well aware that most of them wake with a joie de vivre that never ceases to perplex. They can go to sleep at three in the morning and toss and turn for 4 hours only to wake like the world is a theme park and they have been gifted a free ticket. I am by no means old, but I am also very conscious of my lack of this kind of dangerous energy so early in the day. I have learned the hard way that as an adult, it leads to over-commitments, extensions that are almost always regretted as the day wears on.

Each child carries their own clothes down the stairs to the living room and the ones that can dress themselves begin to do so. The smallest cannot consistently get dressed in a timely manner, and while I appreciate the strategy of letting kids struggle to achieve their dreams, I don't have time to watch a three-year-old work at a shirt for twenty minutes while the others are already on their way to sledding. I put down the baby and dress the three-year-old, stopping every so often to ensure the baby hasn't found some random piece of old food or garbage on my living room rug to choke on. This makes it sound like I live in a certain level of filth and that is completely accurate. I have four children, a husband, and a dog. Cleanliness is a goal that appears very far down the list of things I hope to achieve on a daily basis.

The kids are all dressed and making their way to the back door to find their snow suits. Before I can give instructions, the five-year-old is already wearing boots and a jacket, even though snow pants are the obvious first item of clothing. She must remove the boots and coat. She is not pleased at these counterproductive instructions. Seven-year-old is now digging through the snow pants bin, throwing all pairs that are not his onto the floor. Turns out, his snow pants are hanging by the stove, so the mess was completely unnecessary. I can't find the other kids' snow pants now because they are at the bottom of a pile. Three-year-old takes priority, so the baby is placed in a highchair, restrained and occupied with a snack. He looks on in delight as the volume begins to rise.

Three-year-old has bumps in his socks, which did not bother him three minutes ago, but now are no longer acceptable. He must have new socks immediately. Thankfully, he declares that he is not afraid of the monsters, so he runs off to find more socks. While he is gone, I find the snow pants for the five-year-old and we begin to shimmy them onto her body. The straps are too tight, which causes some flustered and breathless whining, but this situation is figured out quickly. With snow pants on, we move to the boots. They go on easily but then are instantly rejected because they don't feel good. We take them off and hold them upside down. Sure enough, a matchbox car rolls out of one and a handful of dog food from the other. The boots go back on. They feel good this time. We move to the jacket. But not the green one that is supposed to be hers. That one is too big in the arms, she says. She wants to wear the three-year-old's jacket instead, which means that his snow pants won't cut it, he needs a full body snowsuit. That is thankfully fine, and he is not yet back from the sock hunt to have an opinion on the matter. The smaller blue jacket goes onto the five-year-old and the gloving begins.

This is my least favorite part of the whole ordeal.

It takes at least 10 minutes.

For some reason, children do not have full understanding of their beautifully opposable thumbs when it comes to fitting them into the finger holes of gloves and mittens. I hold the glove up and ask the five-year-old to slide her hand in, she instead waits for me to push the glove onto her hand. I don't fight it. I begin to wiggle the glove onto her hand but instead of holding the hand rigid, it becomes an al dente noodle, wobbling and moving away from the glove's pressure.

I take several deep breaths and explain that one must push into a glove for the glove to go over one's fingers. Please push against the pressure of the glove, I say, trying hard to hide my exasperation. She finally does and the glove slips on. The fingers go where they should and my relief is palpable. The second glove goes on even more easily and we're off to the races. She does not want a hat and that's fine with me. There are more pressing issues. I do not know where my three-year-old is and he has been out of ear shot for an uncomfortable period of time. The baby is given another snack and a kiss on the head and the five-year-old is pushed out the door with a grin on her face. The seven-year-old is now searching for mittens and while his frenzied search is anxiety-inducing, I must ask him to watch the baby while I find the three-year-old who is now undoubtedly not just looking for socks.

Three-year-old has emptied the sock bin in his sister's dresser looking for his socks, which have never been located in his sister's dresser. When his search produced no results, he switched gears to something more entertaining. Not that surprising. He is smashing cars together at the top of the stairs. The "losers" litter the steps and I notice this only after the tender arch of my left foot has landed squarely on the pink jeep. The kids named this particular car "The Guppie." My irritation flares, but to be honest, it is difficult to remain upset at an inanimate object called The Guppie.

I find his socks, ask him to get on my back for a piggyback ride to the back door as I glance wearily at the mess that we will have to clean up together later. Now is not the time. The baby is with a seven-year-old who is definitely not watching him.

Back at the mitten bin, the oldest has found some gloves and is asking for help in tucking them into the sleeves of his jacket. He also needs the snow pant leg bands to be pulled over his boots so the snow can't get it while he plays. Both tasks are completed with little fuss and the seven-year-old is sent out the door to find his sister in the snow.

I am left with a baby and a three-year-old. The baby is getting fussy, so I pick him up and attempt to get a three-year-old into a full body snowsuit with one hand. Not happening.

Snow Day

The baby goes on the floor near the boots and will surely begin putting them into his mouth, but if I'm fast, I can get the three-year-old outside before too many germs have been consumed. The full body snowsuit goes on fast, and the boots too. But it is too much to hope the gloving will proceed without incident. I hear they make fake gloves for kids with only a small divot for the thumb and a mitten-like pouch for the fingers. I don't have these. I have mittens with a tiny thumb hole or gloves with a tiny thumb hole.

This ordeal begins with me asking the three-year-old where his thumb is. He holds up his pointer finger without fail. No, I say, it's not that one. Then his middle finger comes up. This gesture, while resonating deeply with how I feel about mittens, must be ignored with casual indifference. Children have an intuitive sense about these things. The slightest indication that a gesture or phrase has a hidden meaning and you've sentenced yourself to a multitude of ill-timed and humiliating future incidents. Nope. Not that one either. As tired as I am, I can't deny how adorable this child is while trying to identify a finger we discuss on a regular basis, and which is used for the common gesture of "thumbs up." We get to the bottom of the thumb question with some humor. Now we can attempt the mittens.

The baby has some dog food in his fists, so I dig it out and move him to a walking device that rolls around the kitchen, allowing him access to the silverware cabinet, which he will certainly empty, but this will buy me enough time for this last step.

The three-year-old has developed a complete lack of ability to hold his arms with rigidity and so they flop and wiggle while I shove them into a tiny mitten. The thumb misses the thumb hole and he looks up at me with utter shock and delight. It missed! For some reason this is a game to him, one in which there is no shame or displeasure at missing the thumb hole. For me, it is a race against time. If I don't get him dressed within the next five minutes, he will overheat and begin panicking. The older kids might decide they're done playing and come into the house, ruining his chances at being one of the big kids. We have to work fast. I shove his hand a second time into the mitten. Thumb misses. He looks up with big eyes and a smile. Missed again Mama! I beg him to hold his thumb apart from the other fingers. He makes a fist. No no. Not like that, I show him my fingers grouped together tightly with a thumb sticking out to the side. He tries it, but when I try to push the mitten on, he does not let his thumb go in, he holds it stiff and unyielding, even to the mitten entrance. I can hear laughter. The sleds have been located and the older kids are now zipping joyfully down the hill in the yard. I beg him to try harder at getting his hand into the mitten. Now he's looking concerned. I'm flustered. He wants to go outside. A loud crash comes from the kitchen where the baby has emptied the plastic silverware drawer onto the floor.

The first mitten finally goes on and the whole charade happens again with his second hand. I did not exaggerate when I said the mitten phase of dressing takes ten minutes to complete. But we get it done and the three-year-old is sent out the door to find his siblings.

I hold hope that I may drink two or three sips of coffee before being asked to complete any more parenting tasks, but cannot bring myself to leave the baby in his seat a minute longer, as he has been largely ignored for going on thirty minutes. His good nature has saved all of our lives, but I don't like taking advantage of it. I pick him up and snuggle him with one arm while collecting the spoons and forks from the floor and putting them back in their bin. Might a child use one of these utensils without it being washed? Absolutely. I am certain there are many people in this world who would be horrified to know this is the case. I am not one of them. Will a child get sick because their fork sat on my kitchen floor for five minutes and I put it back in the clean bin? Very unlikely. Sure, in an ideal world I might give my kids clean utensils every time they eat, but in an ideal world, my children also wouldn't eat things they find in the forest or down at the pond. The system isn't perfect.

As a Mainer, I have fully accepted that the winter months present unique challenges. Shoveling driveways and front steps, the endless shuffle of wood from wetter piles to drier piles and eventually into the kitchen to drip and dry by the roaring wood stove. While the physicality of these tasks is undeniable, the snow day elicits a dread so heavy it hurts my bones.

There is a knock at the back door. It has been 17 minutes. The kids want to come back in. As I open the door, the snow begins to drop from the snow pants and boots all over the floor. They do not pay attention to the boundaries of the welcome mats. Boots are kicked off, mittens flung to the floor. All of that effort stripped off and discarded in seconds. Snow begins to melt into pools. Rosy cheeks and smiles are asking for hot cocoa and toast. I hang the wet things on the fence around the wood stove to dry. They will certainly be used again today, maybe even within the hour, to go out on another wintery foray. I may even be the one to help the kids get dressed again, if I am not dead from exhaustion.

Today on the Farm: Broken Pocket

My kids love pockets. Secret pockets are best, as I think we can all agree, but all pockets are appreciated and heavily utilized in our house. Need to hide a prune? Pocket. Need to keep a baby snake comfortable? Pocket. Need a place to stash a beautiful rock you stole from your sister? Pocket. So, it should not surprise me that when one of these pockets malfunctions, it will be reported immediately. But I think I'm getting ahead of myself. It might be worth first describing the exact parameters of what makes something a pocket. A pocket begins with an opening in an otherwise solid piece of material, I think that much is obvious. For me personally, the next qualification would be that the opening in the material must lead to an area separated from other areas and able to hold something. This is where my notion of pockets diverge from Oggie's.

Today I spent a good twenty minutes trying to describe why the hole in his shirt where his head goes is not a pocket. He kept sticking his hand into the opening at his neck and then dropping things in. When items fell to the floor from the bottom of his shirt, he complained that the pocket was broken. It didn't matter how many times I tried to reason with him that the neck hole did not in fact qualify as a pocket, he disagreed. His hand could go in and so could his rocks and toys, so it was a pocket. A terribly broken one.

Spa Day

There comes a time, after having moved the woodpile to its seventh location, that a little relaxation is warranted. It was a happy coincidence that Nathan's family recognized this same fact during the week that he and I both turned 40. As a birthday gift to the two of us, they generously all chipped in and paid for a couples' day at the spa.

Let me dispel any immediate misconceptions. I am not a person who regularly visits spas. In fact, I had never stepped foot in a spa prior to this experience, and neither had Nathan. Our general ineptitude and country bumpkin status was almost instantly apparent. Let me also say that despite the foibles that transpired on the day of our scheduled relaxation, it was an overall positive experience and if you are a spa person, I hold you in the same regard I hold all other humans prior to getting to know them.

We left our children at the agreed upon time in the agreed upon place to leisurely make our way to the spa, which was located in a beautiful city I will refrain from disclosing. On the drive, Nathan and I became concerned that if we arrived at a spa at 9:00 am and our massages (part of the gift) were not until 1:30 pm, we would have no idea what to do with ourselves for such an extended period of time. There were swimming pools and hot tubs, but I do not particularly enjoy being wet. Nathan doesn't mind it, but I think the idea of me choosing a different activity at the spa than him was, to him, horrifying. He didn't say as much, but I got the distinct impression he considered himself in enemy territory and without companionship, would have abandoned the whole affair and lied about having ever gone at all.

We found a coffee shop along the way and spent as long as possible eating our bagels and gluten-free breakfast wraps. The coffee was good, and therefore gone too soon. There was no choice but to continue. The beautiful city that housed the spa was too small to spend hours exploring and too crowded with tourists to find a place to read a book or write, which were the activities Nathan and I most wanted to do on our day of freedom.

When we arrived at the spa, the anxiety in the car was palpable. To avoid going directly to the door, Nathan argued that there might be more appropriate parking spots at the resort than in the lot adjacent to a giant sign that read, "SPA PARKING." We drove around a bit and so as not to make the walk too short, Nathan chose a lot up the hill from the very clearly marked entrance.

For better or worse, there is an image that comes to mind when I try to picture a person who regularly visits the spa. Namely, I envision an individual who places a premium on physical cleanliness and emotional wellbeing. Part of me wishes I was this kind of person. It's not that Nathan and I don't value being clean, or desire to be well-adjusted humans who take care of themselves. It's that those things feel like stretch goals right now. We are not particularly clean or well balanced. We are living in utter madness. If we can bathe our four children enough times to keep their bedsheets clean for a week, we're in good shape. Often that means the water is no longer hot and we don't have the energy to scrub the dirt from ourselves.

I agreed not to leave Nathan alone to fend for himself in a spa pool or a dimly lit hot tub with whomever else might be relaxing. While we recognized that we were "spa-goers" we also recognized that almost every other person at the spa seemed legitimately relaxed, whereas we were both extremely tense and uncomfortable with our own lack of experience and knowledge in the realm of appropriate spa behavior.

We wandered around "exploring" for almost 30 minutes, unable to choose a location to sit and relax because it was too quiet or too loud or too sunny and we hadn't relaxed since 2012, so we had forgotten how. When you have small kids there is a period of unwinding that has to happen to enjoy life away from those kids for any amount of time. Nathan claims he would need at least three weeks to fully unwind and so accepts that he may not reach a state of relaxation for the next 17 to 25 years.

To be quite honest, I think I could have unwound in about 35 minutes if I were by myself at the spa. But to sit next to my husband, who I know was deeply uncomfortable with the entire concept of spas, who was watching in dismay as people donned robes that were worn by other people and slippers that were communal, wondering how much clothing he should wear under his robe when fetched by a masseuse, is not relaxing. I could not help but absorb all of that tension and horror and sit at a level of about 5% relaxation in a wicker chair with wet cushions and no table on which to place my laptop.

This state of discomfort continued for a number of hours while we were waiting for our allotted massage time. About an hour before 1:30, we decided to get acquainted with the lounges, which had been explained as mere waiting rooms from which the masseuses would fetch us. There was a women's lounge and a men's, and while I cannot speak to the quality of the men's, I will tell you that the women's lounge is where I should have been the entire morning. It had beautiful furniture, tables, fluffy pillows, and not a soul was sitting in the space. It would have been a lovely location to settle down to write.

But to say that the lounge was merely a place from which to be fetched was highly inaccurate. It became clear almost immediately that there were procedures that had not been explained. There were lockers with robes within them, there were signs mandating slippers that were nowhere to be found. There were rooms behind rooms where quiet voices could be heard and it was impossible to determine whether rounding a corner would result in an embarrassing encounter with a completely naked stranger looking for privacy.

I had to ask a young woman who appeared to be moving towels where I was and what I needed to do to open a locker and arm myself with slippers. I accidentally washed my hands with mouthwash because there was a mouthwash dispenser next to the sink in addition to a soap dispenser. I did my best, but it's very difficult to make it look like you are washing your hands on purpose with spearmint mouthwash. I marveled at the complementary hair gel and aerosolized deodorant and numerous other shower accessories. I tried to imagine a situation in which I would need these items and expect to be provided with them. The spa lounge was a fancy hotel room stocked with every imaginable complimentary toiletry and also some unimaginable ones.

I stripped down and wrapped myself in a robe, then found a chaise to wait on. As promised, the masseuse arrived and her lilting voice invited me to follow her down a meandering set of hallways and steps. I can't say for sure, but I believe she took me all the way to the basement. As we walked in silence, I imagined Nathan being taken on a similar journey. I hoped that for him it wasn't triggering memories of his only other "professional" massage, which had been given by a reformed female Thai prisoner during our travels in Southeast Asia. We had been separated just prior to that massage as well. The experience in Thailand left him with nerve impairment and a fear of being abandoned in tight spaces with women offering massage. I could only imagine how he would feel as his masseuse escorted him to the bowels of the building where no one could hear his screams. Thankfully, the spa provided more training than the Thai prison reform system and aside from Nathan walking into the situation endearingly uninformed and causing a bit of a scene, he felt the experience did him some good. My massage was delightful and I experienced no complications.

After our massages, we made our way to the resort restaurant where our dinner was paid for in full and we ate and laughed the way I assume normal people do when they're relaxing at the spa.

I can guarantee that in the future, if a spa day is organized, Nathan will remain home to read his book in the bright sun of our own backyard. He will likely remain fully clothed and spend almost no time worrying about it being too loud or too quiet. I will be at the spa, brushing my teeth, rinsing with fancy mouthwash, washing my hands with actual soap, and writing my next book in the lounge. Completely alone.

For the Birds

About ten years ago, Nathan and I were traveling in Singapore. We stumbled upon an absolutely enormous aviary. Nathan was instantly interested in spending a day there. I was not. I thought most birds were exactly the same, but that some were bigger, dirtier, and more hideous than others. Nathan too was ignorant of most things bird. He, at his own admission, called all birds he didn't know nut hatches. I didn't even go that far. The only differentiation I made between bird species was, edible and not socially acceptable as edible.

If you are a birder, you will find some of my previously held beliefs appalling. I will be the first to admit that I was unenlightened. This is the caliber birder I am: I can identify a starling and a brown headed cowbird. I know the difference between a downy woodpecker and a hairy woodpecker. I can easily identify female rose-breasted grosbeaks and evening grosbeaks, but I have trouble differentiating between warblers of all kinds and I can't reliably identify a cedar waxwing or tell the difference between a house finch and a purple finch.

If you're not a birder, this list may feel exhausting to read and you might be questioning whether you're going to keep reading this essay. I assure you, I'm almost done naming birds. If you're a birder though, you've just discovered I hover very low on the totem pole of people who know things about birds. That said, my knowledge about them is only tangentially important to the real meat of what I have to say on this topic.

I can't say for sure where my distaste for birds came from, but my instinct is to blame it all on my parents. I'm coming to appreciate this tendency from a new perspective as I am now the parent of four people who have already begun to blame me for things for which I cannot possibly be responsible. Bottom line, my mother is a little neurotic when it comes to birds. She hates them. I don't think she hates looking at them, it's more a fear of being attacked by them, but this was not a distinction my adolescent brain cared to make. When I was young, to touch a bird feather was to touch disease and almost certain death if hands were not washed immediately. This mentality became deeply seeded in my psyche and continued with me into adulthood. In my recollections, my father never expressed a feeling on birds one way or the other. Sometimes he'd save a nest instead of running it over with his tractor to let the baby birds hatch and grow, but that seemed a common act of decency toward a living creature, not a statement of appreciation for the birds themselves.

Back to Singapore. Nathan had to bribe me to spend four hours at the most spectacular aviary you could imagine. I don't remember what the bribe was, but there were a couple of things that come to mind as having been important to me during that time. One was the pastries and assorted desert trays in the Indian market. The second was a shopping center I'd been meaning to visit but hadn't been able to convince Nathan to keep me company. He must have promised one or both of these things because we spent the afternoon looking at birds and for reasons beyond my comprehension, I was tasked with photographing them. In many of my pictures, the birds appear well to the side of the frame and the apparent subject of the photos is always something obnoxiously mundane like a bench or a trash can. It was an unfortunate and rather juvenile act of rebellion. I see that now. But to the credit of Photoshop, I can crop all those old pictures if I ever want to.

I think I've provided enough of a background to make one thing painfully clear. I had to undergo a significant transition from who I was to someone who sits in front of their kitchen window trying to determine how a chipping sparrow looks different than a song sparrow. This transition occurred slowly and without intention. It occurred how I imagine many transformations happen to parents of children with hobbies and interests of their own. I was trying to stay relevant. Attempting to share in the excitement of my three oldest kids as they learned the easy birds first. And it turned out, I could tell a goldfinch from a chickadee too. I wasn't a complete ignoramus.

And then, as the list grew of the birds my five-year-old could identify, so did mine. And as my seven-year-old learned amazing facts about the chickadee, so did I. Did you know that the chickadee's warning call is the one that sounds like, "Chicka-dee dee dee dee"? And that the more "dees" the greater the danger? These birds have a sliding scale for threat assessment. Our dog Tulip is on the higher end of that scale, as indicated by the "dee dee dee-ing" that happens every time she's let out of the house.

When my kids scream excitedly at the living room window that they see a new bird, I am right there with them, trying to pick out unique features to compare to pictures in our Sibley's bird book and the Sibley's bird app on my phone. You read that correctly. I have a bird identification app on my smartphone.

The thing is, I have come to understand a little something about myself while sitting perfectly still, staring at the five feeders we have hanging by the lilac tree. When I was a child, I felt strongly that our family owned the land we lived on. It was ours. We worked it and it provided. I was too self-centered to see the physical world with more nuance. These birds are teaching my kids (and me) that none of it—the land, the fruit, the animals—are ours. We are coexisting and it is our responsibility to sit still and wonder at the beauty of it all.

These birds are important. They are teaching this family to love the diversity and magic of nature. By sitting still and quiet we are practicing the art of noticing. It takes patience to see the color of a bird's throat as it flits from branch to feeder to ground. It takes stepping outside of one's own desire to move and go and do into a place of offering. We are acknowledging to ourselves there is more to being alive than what we wish to take from it. Isn't this an offering of ourselves to the openness of awe? To know birds is to know a little about how unbelievably unique and delicate nature can be. And how complicated and fierce.

Last month we saw two new species of warbler on their migratory route to the Taiga. The whole house was in an uproar as we excitedly argued about which colors we'd seen on which feathers. We searched our books and my app and scoured the Internet for the list of birds who'd been overhead in their migrations the night before. My children were researchers and scientists. When we thought we'd figured it out, they sat for almost an hour at the window, hoping another visitor would stop in to refuel. While they waited, I can only speculate at where their marvelous imaginations brought them. Also while they waited, I took deep breaths of appreciation for these children. Because of them, I have grown into a person who is working toward warblers and cedar waxwings. Nathan no longer disrespects the nut hatches. He notices whether they're white-breasted or rose-breasted and makes sure the suet is plentiful enough to sustain them.

Today on the Farm: Skunks

To explain what happened today on the farm, I am going to have to explain what happened yesterday and the day before that. It has been an unsavory few days. The trouble started when Jack decided to trap the animal knocking down and eating the birdseed from beneath our feeders at night.

No. That's not entirely true.

It started when Jack got a game camera for Christmas.

No. Not true either.

It started when Jack was born eight years ago. Jack is a product of generations of Neves and I blame all of us for the way this week has unfolded.

Sometimes when one parent is annoyed at the other, they say things like, "You won't believe what YOUR son did." That is amusing because obviously they share responsibility for producing their offspring. But I swear, the genes in this child come directly from a generation before mine on the Neves side. I couldn't pull off the "YOUR son" line with a straight face. Jack is every goodhearted, curious, determined, dangerously irreverent, meddlesome Neves that came before him.

When Jack decides he's going to do something, he does it. So when the birdseed started disappearing in the wee hours, and the birds weren't getting their breakfasts, Jack resolved to handle it. He propped his new game camera on a stick by the feeder and left it overnight to capture the thief. The next morning, we uploaded the images from the memory card onto a laptop to see what had been lurking the night before.

The game camera snaps a picture every 3 seconds if it is triggered by its motion sensor to do so. Images started showing activity around 2 a.m. At first, mostly mice darting back and forth. Then, a flash or two of a large cat appeared. We don't have a cat. Our neighbors don't have a cat. This was an exciting intruder indeed. Jack intended to catch it and even though he didn't verbalize it, he was likely hoping we could keep it. As a side note, it was absolutely obvious to all of us that a cat was not stealing bird seed. A cat was hunting mice, who were stealing bird seed. The real culprits were of the rodent variety, and this cat was doing us a favor, but Jack was heading down a path that had everything to do with catching a new pet and nothing to do with solving our real problem.

Jack called my father to ask if he could borrow his large live trap. My father always feigns surprise at the chaos around here, but in truth, he does as much as possible to supply Jack with the proper tools to instigate it. The trap was delivered immediately.

This brings us to two nights ago.

Jack set his trap within close proximity to the feeder and to the house. That night, the trap was sprung. Good fortune smiled upon us all that I happened to peek out the window in the living room just prior to letting out our hunting dog, Tulip, for her morning constitutional. The house went from slow and sleepy to insanity. The kids' screams of excitement and terror filled the house. The skunk could hear them through the windows and began to twitch its hindquarters in our direction, as if to say, "You're making me nervous."

Catching a skunk is not uncommon in the country. They like the apples that fall from trees in autumn, they like compost heaps, they like when your lawn is full of grubs. They steal cat food and apparently, bird seed. Knowing this does not mitigate the fear one feels when one realizes they now possess a frightened skunk in a metal cage that must be removed without being upset in any way.

There is a trick that anyone who has ever successfully moved a skunk without frightening it will tell you. You must blind the skunk to its surroundings. It seems counterintuitive that taking away an animal's ability to see a threat coming would calm it down, but there you have it. I handed Nathan a very large towel and expressed how strongly I believed in him. Nathan is not a morning person. Assigning him this task was truly one of the riskiest things I have ever done.

In gigantic boots, which I found to be a very poor choice in the arena of stealth, Nathan clambered around the house to approach the skunk in such a way as to be blocked from sight by the trap's solid door. Good fortune smiled upon us again when he was able to carefully lay the towel over the cage without upsetting its inhabitant. This move was followed by a very slow walk, trap in hand, to the back of our Subaru where a plastic sheet was placed and the cage set gingerly atop it.

Nathan and I drove the skunk together to a release location which we believed was far enough away from other human domiciles to go unnoticed. The skunk reluctantly left the trap when it was opened and we returned home with signs of relief and annoyance, as this had all transpired before our morning coffee.

That would have been the end of it, if it weren't for the genetic material of Neves sputtering encouragement within the deepest cells of Jack's 8-year-old brain. He hadn't caught the cat.

I don't know for certain why neither Nathan or I thought to advise Jack about a few important things before bed last night. Namely that traps should be set a safe distance from the house and that when you catch one skunk, you might catch another one. And I don't know why we went to bed without realizing that Jack wasn't finished yet.

This brings us to today on the farm.

This morning, much like yesterday morning, we awoke to a trap containing an irritated skunk. The kids were again delighted. I was already calculating the distance between myself and caffeine. It wasn't looking good. I had an idea of how long it was going to take Nathan to get up and mentally prepare for this whole charade again, so I decided to take the first part of the operation into my own hands. I grabbed the same bath towel and headed around the house on the same route Nathan had taken yesterday. I wore small boots and stepped lightly. As I approached the cage, the skunk shifted ever so slightly and became aware of my presence. I froze. It froze. We looked into each other's eyes and in that split-second, decisions were made. The skunk decided to warn me. I decided that if I were being warned, I might as well get the towel on the cage.

Here is something about a skunk's spray that the average person might not know: At first, a skunk's spray smells a little sweet. Almost pleasant. This feeling lasts for about two seconds inside your nose. While you are getting the first whiffs, you think you are lucky that it was only a little bit of spray because it isn't very strong. You are almost always wrong.

The skunk in the cage did not give me a tiny warning poof. It sprayed our house and the ground and the cage and in the moment the odor fully matured within my nostrils I began to dry heave while my children watched through the window. I ran away as fast as I could, hoping I had not been struck directly.

This is the point at which Nathan became aware of the situation. The bedroom window is situated on the second floor, just above the now extremely agitated and odiferous skunk. When I returned through the back door the children ran away from me, shrieking in every direction. As quickly as possible I stripped out of my clothes and threw them out of the house. It was difficult to determine at this point whether I was the one who smelled, or if it was the smell seeping through the side of the house, through cracks in windows, or through the basement floorboards. The house was filled with screams of disgust at the blossoming odor of onion and dirty feet. Nathan raced down the stairs and bumped into me, running in the opposite direction, completely naked. To say he was surprised would be understating it. As I flew up the stairs for fresh garb, I heard Nathan scream, "What the hell is going on down here?"

We regrouped as soon as I was clothed. The kids called a family meeting. They begged us to get the thing off the property as soon as possible. We were obviously in agreement that immediate action was necessary.

Nathan and I searched the recesses of our morning brains for an idea, any idea that did not involve the Subaru. None came. The clock was ticking. Despite it being a sub-optimal plan, we were forced to load the cage, towel, and skunk, which were all emitting nauseatingly potent skunk odor, into the trunk.

I'd like to pause to say that this is where I think we could have really improved the outcome of this debacle. While I admit that I was the one to initiate the first warning spray, I don't think I was the one to push us past the point of no return. That was Nathan.

When the skunk had been loaded into the car, Nathan stood by the open trunk signaling silently for me to get into the car with him. It was understandable for him to feel that I should also have to endure the punishment of my poor technique. I opened the passenger door as quietly as I could and slid my body into the seat. Just as I was muffling the sound of my own clicking buckle, Nathan did the unspeakable. He slammed the trunk door down, momentarily forgetting what was inside. My eyes widened in horror and disbelief and as one might expect, the car began to fill with a dense fog. The spray was so thick I had to open the door to throw my body, still strapped in, as far out into the fresh air as possible. There was no fresh air. The world was now contaminated and my lungs burned in shock and pain. My eyes watered. My guts twisted and I was thankful I hadn't yet had breakfast. Nathan sheepishly entered the driver's side door and waited for my gagging to stop. We made eye contact and I mouthed a few expletives in his direction. We didn't dare talk because while it seemed impossible that the situation could get any worse, it also seemed prudent not to test it.

We pulled out of the driveway with all of the windows down and our heads as far out of them as possible. For the duration of the drive, Nathan and I took turns dry heaving, laughing, and crying. Let me pause again to say that if you think you understand or relate to this story because you have smelled a skunk as you've driven by a spot one has sprayed, or you've caught a whiff of one on a walk through the woods, you are sorely mistaken. This kind of casual interaction with skunk odor is common and extremely misleading.

I have never really respected skunks. I always thought they were adorable forest creatures with a cute little defense mechanism to frighten away predators. Truth is, these beasts *are* the predators. In my life, no odor has come close to causing the physical discomfort I felt in the car this morning. I may have been crying and laughing but don't let that fool you. Being trapped in an enclosed space with a skunk who has just sprayed feels life threatening. You are about to die because your lungs refuse to pull breath. It is a dry drowning.

If you Google, "What does skunk spray smell like?" you will get answers like, "It smells a little like onions or garlic because it contains the same thiol compound," or "a little sulfury." But in a Subaru, a skunk's spray smells like rotten onions and garlic and eggs and decaying carrion ground up into a paste and shoved directly into your brain by way of your face.

The situation did not improve when we were able to jump out of the car at the designated release spot. Feeling we had nothing to lose, Nathan quickly opened the trunk to grab the trap. Life lesson: There is always something to lose.

Hearing the trunk open, the skunk became agitated again, waves of fresh odor engulfed Nathan as he grabbed the trap and quickly moved it to an open spot in the field, holding his breath all the way. When the trap was open, he snuck back to the road to wait for the skunk to leave so we could grab the trap and get home. The creature was in no hurry. For ten minutes we sat in the chilly morning air, waiting. When it finally began to rustle around, the skunk somehow set the trap off for a second time, slamming the metal door down with a clatter. What little was left within its tiny stink pouch was released.

Rolling his eyes in exasperation, Nathan tip-toed back to the trap, opened it again, and backed away a second time. Eventually the skunk decided to take its leave, trotting away with a self-satisfied shuffle step.

Nathan and I drove home with our heads out the windows again and instead of pulling into the driveway, we drove straight up into the back field and opened the windows, doors and trunk. The car will remain there until the smell dissipates. The smell inside the house has improved slightly, but I will be going out to try and battle the scene of the crime with some white vinegar later today.

As for the effort to capture the creatures stealing our birdseed, Jack has been instructed to cease and desist, at least for now.

A Helper

There is little in this world that brings Oggie more pleasure than being helpful. When someone is in need of assistance, he is always the first one to offer information, guidance, instruction. As his parents, Nathan and I understand there is often a disconnect between Oggie's willingness to help and his ability to help. After all, he is only three.

Not long ago, Nathan's parents came to visit. They are wonderful people and fantastic grandparents. When they're here, they spend lots of time at the pond with the kids. They join in when the kids are catching frogs, fishing, kayaking. At the house, they read books, play chess, and organize elaborate tea parties that always turn out to be complete disasters, but are loved by all. As wonderful as Nathan's parents are with the kids, it should be acknowledged that they have not been around children other than ours since Nathan and his brother were little. Therefore, they are sometimes caught off guard by reality as it applies to individuals who are not yet grown. Reality, some might argue is the same no matter how old you are. It is reality. This argument falls short when you're living with kids. Reality is not reality to a person who is three.

Oggie's reality is that he identifies as helpful.

When Grampa began complaining of a lost shoe, Oggie appeared, exuding complete confidence that he could sort things out. It just so happened that he had seen the missing shoe and was thrilled to share that information.

"Oh, I know where that shoe is," he offered. "It's on the roof of our house."

A Helper

This news came as a bit of a shock to Grampa, who had last seen his shoe in the mud room. Despite how little sense it made for a shoe to be on a roof, Grampa exhibited only the slightest suspicion because he has seen a thing or two around here. As if sensing a bit of trepidation, Oggie boosted his credibility by explaining *how* the shoe had gotten to the roof.

"Jack threw it there."

Enough said.

Grampa exited the house and began scanning the roofline for his shoe. He circled three times, then four. After watching Grampa pass the kitchen window for the fourth time, I couldn't contain my curiosity. I opened the back door to find him discussing the situation with Oggie.

"So which side of the house did he throw it on?"

"He threw it as hard as he could. It just disappeared!"

"Where was he standing when he threw my shoe?"

"On the ground."

This last answer had me laughing under my breath. It had taken me all of about five seconds to assess what was really going on, but I didn't have the heart to inform Grampa in the presence of his assistant. Instead, I asked, "Grampa, have you lost something?"

"Yes, Oggie says my shoe is on the roof. We've been walking around the house, but I can't seem to find it."

Nathan arrived on the scene, catching the last little bit of the conversation. It was clear from his smirk that he too had figured out exactly what was happening. He said, "Huh. Oggie, can you run around one more time to check the other side of the house?"

As soon as Oggie was out of sight, Nathan turned to Grampa, "Your shoe is not on the roof."

"Oggie said he saw Jack throw it there."

"Oggie says a lot of things. He likes to help."

A Helper

"So where is my shoe?"

"Where's the last place you saw it?"

"The mud room."

"I'd start there."

Oggie ran back around the house, pleased to have again been a useful member of the search party. He delightedly shared that he still had not seen the shoe.

Grampa held out his hand to Oggie and said, "Let's go check the mud room one more time. Just in case Jack put it back."

Sure enough, the shoe was in the mud room.

After Oggie had gone to bed that night, Grampa relayed the whole story to Gramma, who got a huge kick out of the absurdity of it all. She asked questions like, "Why would Jack throw your shoe on the roof?" to which Grampa, in mock irritation exclaimed, "Why does anyone do anything around here?!"

We all had a laugh at how sweet and misguided Oggie's sense of usefulness was. It was impossible not to love everything about this character trait, no matter how fanciful and inaccurate his information.

The next day, Gramma offered to help clean up the yard a bit with some raking. She couldn't find the rake. You can guess who knew where it was. Despite having been forewarned about situations exactly like the one she was experiencing, Gramma followed right behind Oggie as he trotted off to the barn.

I found them there about twenty minutes after they'd entered. They'd been wandering around together and it was unclear who was leading who. From the entrance of the barn I heard Gramma asking, "So, which of these rooms do your parents keep the rake in?"

A Helper

"Well, they keep it in all of the rooms sometimes. But I think...maybe near the chainsaws." Oggie grabbed Gramma's hand, but made no effort to walk anywhere. He was waiting for her.

"Where do they keep the chainsaws?"

"I'm not supposed to touch chainsaws."

This line of questioning was dead, and Gramma stood there, stumped. I yelled from the door of the barn, "Hey Gramma, what is it you two are looking for? Chainsaws?"

"No. No. Oggie said the rake was in here. We've gone in every room and looked behind lots of boards and bikes. We can't find it."

I smiled at Oggie. "Thanks for helping Gramma buddy. I've got it from here."

I whispered to Gramma, "He doesn't know where the rake is. He was just trying to be helpful."

Gramma started to laugh. She'd been had, just like Grampa.

As we all exited the barn, I shared, "I think the rake is leaned up against the side of the house."

Gramma brushed the bat guano and dust from her pants and Oggie raced off ahead, to see if he could find it for her.

Battleground

December 18, 2020

There is a silent war being waged in thousands of farmhouses all over Maine this and every winter. Many a story has been written about the lives lost, the property damage, the drama. It's unlikely this story will inspire improved techniques in battle strategy, or in truth, improvements to anything at all. I can only hope that sharing (with humility) my experiences in this arena will, in a moment of darkness and despair, bring a fellow farm owner solace. The kind that comes with solidarity and maybe even a hint of gloating that one's own situation isn't THAT bad.

Things are worse than bad here. Today I am tired. If I were more energetic, I might be doing something other than writing about my problems. I might be buying gummy bears in bulk. Not to binge-eat my sorrows away, though I am not above such an activity. It is because during extensive first-in-mouse trials, it has become abundantly clear that gummy bears are the most effective bait. I could name a brand of gummy bear that appears to provide superior allure, but I'm not in the business of advertisement or frankly, defamation lawsuits. Let's just say, the more fragrant gummy brands are the most appealing to pinkies and their parents.

I've tried cookies (many brands), peanut butter (smooth only), and various other crumb niblets from meals and snacks. But it is gummy bears that bring the mice to the traps. So far this fall we removed a total of 33 mice from our home before allowing a false sense of superiority to lull us into complacency. If you know anything about mice, you know that they are just waiting for complacency. They are sitting in their little holes, full of your birdseed and the chicken feed you have in your pantry because your seven-year-old thought he needed some for a squirrel trap so he brought it into the house and never moved it back to the barn. The smart mice are snacking happily on the items they collected from your food stores while you eliminated their competition. The smart mice are watching your face as you set the traps, noting your delight every time another of their slower, less capable buddies gets locked in the live trap and taken for a ride. They're biding their time.

When December rolls around, it's natural to feel that 33 mice removed is quite possibly a state record. It's natural to walk around the house, peeking into pantries and cupboards with a self-congratulatory smirk. No crumbs there! No mouse droppings on that shelf! Things are looking great for the holiday season, aren't they?

Wrong.

This slackening of focus is exactly what the smart mice are waiting for. Sure, you'd like to argue the point that a mouse brain, which weighs in at an average of .4 grams, can't possibly impress. I would have likely agreed with you before living in a farmhouse. Now I know better. If mice were the kind of foe most people would like to believe they are, I submit that people would have won by now.

February 6, 2021

It is early February and things are spiraling out of control. Yesterday my curry powder, which is stored in a collection of small tinfoil pouches, was breached. It was the last straw in a series of micro-aggressions I've been trying to ignore. How dare they? I don't know about other people's houses, but in this one, curry powder is valued somewhere between coffee beans and Oreo cookies, which is to say, quite highly.

I've been turning a blind eye for weeks to the small bits of toilet paper fluttering down from the highest shelf in the pantry. Probably just dust, I said to myself, knowing full well what folly that was. Toilet paper doesn't turn to fluffy snowflakes on its own. It takes a mouse. A particularly irreverent brand of mouse, at that. It would have been easy to hide the pilfering of toilet paper, for God's sake—take some from the back of the shelf. But no, in plain view, tiny nibbles are carving their way to the center of not one, but five rolls of tissue all at once. Such spectacular waste. I hesitate to investigate fully because there is a very real possibility that the fluffy white cotton isn't being transported long distances. It is possible the perpetrator lies in wait, mere inches from the evidence. I for one do not relish the idea of a direct confrontation.

I'll digress for a moment and explain that after my victory over mousekind late last year, our most successful live trap was stepped on by a three-year-old and destroyed. I looked to replace it, but all comparable models were sold out. I feared my own mental trajectory—which is predictable and always in the direction of reduced vigilance—so I purchased several knock-off brands. Full disclosure, not all were live traps. In an ideal world, we would have the time and goodwill to take all of our captives for a ride. In the real world, it was December and below freezing and the prospect of de-icing a vehicle at six in the morning to give a joyride to a rodent didn't appeal to anyone. In addition, there are certain farm-related tasks that need to be addressed with truth. I do not wish to do a disservice to the intellect of the reader, who quite possibly has already realized that a relocated mouse is a doomed mouse during certain times of year, including this one. Live traps become inhumane when the mouse has nowhere to go but the snow-covered forest during a Maine winter.

The most useless of the new devices was a contraption claiming the ability to lure a mouse into a small compartment, which was nearly impossible to load with bait. Once there, the mouse was dispatched with speed and would never be seen directly by the homeowner. The directions instructed, simply pick the trap up and throw it away. This trap was distasteful to me for a myriad of reasons, the top two being: First, if you are a cold-hard killer, you should not be permitted the luxury of cowardice, of avoiding the sight of your own inhumanity. Second, the trap was made of plastic, and not a small amount of it. To expect anyone facing the prospect of ridding their home of mice to buy and dispose of so much plastic is ludicrous. Not to mention an assault on our planet. The trap cost almost three dollars. If we'd had to use one for each of our captures, we would have been financially better off feeding the mice all winter with blocks of fancy cheese.

We also bought about a dozen sticky traps, which are, by far, the worst kind of mouse trap. It doesn't take much imagination to reach the horrific conclusion that something must still be done with a live mouse that is stuck in glue. You can't throw it away without first dispatching the mouse and while I talk a good game about facing cowardice and being tough, I pass this job to my husband every single time.

And so, here we are, early February, toilet paper and curry powder being ransacked nightly. The insults are becoming impossible to ignore. Yesterday a mouse ran over my foot as I used the toilet in broad daylight. You can't tell me that wasn't a targeted psychological attack. Broad daylight! These creatures are supposed to be nocturnal. That means there are so many mice that they have begun daring one another to behave like drunkards at a fraternity party.

It was the toilet incident that inspired me to search for, (and find) more of the prized live traps we used last fall. I bought two more. One went into the basement and the other under a couch in the living room. Neither has captured a mouse and I know exactly why. I'm out of gummy bears.

Could I conceivably set a trap with curry powder, or cookies, or frankly any number of other items I know that the mice are eating when the lights go off every evening? Sure, I could. But the mice wouldn't fall for them. Remember, these are the smart ones. They flit from rice bag to pecan sack like the free-spirited thrill seekers they are. They fancy themselves untouchable, because well, they have been.

I'll run to the store this weekend to pick up a wide range of gummy objects. Worms work, bears, even some varieties of gummy fish. But I know myself and my children well enough to know this is a dangerous game. You see, these four small children are also drawn to the fruity perfume that hangs in the air above an open bag of gummy things. If I'm being completely frank, I am not immune to the temptation of an occasional indulgence. This is a race against time—a battle between us and them and between us and ourselves. If we are winning one battle, almost certainly we are losing the other. Too much candy will be consumed by all. The mice will die for their mistake, and although our deaths are far slower and more difficult to process, with each gummy consumed, we are unmistakably moving in that direction.

I can't speak to the exact level of understanding a mouse may or may not have about the human condition. I can only observe that in this battleground, our home, it certainly *seems* like they are using our psychological failings against us.

May 10, 2021

I just cannot live like this anymore. The mice have gone through multiple breeding cycles since my last accounting and the 33 we removed last year have been easily replaced. The day-trotters are now making appearances almost every morning while the kids and I are eating breakfast. I can't remember a morning in the last three weeks where one of us hasn't screamed, "Mouse!"

They're darting under the dishwasher, they're hiding in boots. I found one of Ezra's bibs wrapped around a little pocket of bird seed in a drawer. The insults are mounting. We keep setting our magical live traps, the one responsible for so much success late last year and nothing is happening. The mice have been sharing intel and now, even the most delicious gummy bear, even the organic juice-based ones for God's sake aren't drawing these monsters from the safety of their toilet paper-lined nests.

But my lemonade powder is now all over the cupboard shelves and my decaf coffee (which is hidden deep in the closet lest we accidentally make it when we were aiming to get caffeinated) is contaminated with mouse poop. The Raman noodles are a lost cause, the miso soup I was saving, ruined.

Something serious must be done and I have an idea.

I need to run it through the proper channels.

May 14, 2021

It is settled, we have enacted a house policy. For every mouse or (God forbid) rat that Jack can catch, trap, eliminate, there will be a one-dollar bounty paid. Squirrels and chipmunks, if captured in the basement will fetch a higher price.

Right now, as much as I hate to admit it, Jack is the member of this family who possesses the skill set to get this job done. I haven't slept a full night in 8 years (since my pregnancy with Jack back in 2012) and right now the sleep is particularly bad with a teething baby. I can't stay focused on this situation. Nathan is also not at the top of his game. While I can't speak to his deficiencies in the mouse elimination game with complete confidence, I feel he is lacking the appropriate level of disgust at the assault. Don't get me wrong, he wants the mice gone, but he is not as often faced with their antics as he is not usually the one awake at 5:30 a.m. while they're prancing around the kitchen. He also isn't as concerned as I am about the loss of lemonade and decaf coffee. You can be certain if the mice were pooping in the chips or nibbling the bagels it'd be a different story.

Jack on the other hand is uniquely suited for this chore. It is paid work, which is possibly the greatest draw. As a seven-year-old, it is difficult to make money. There are very few paying jobs for people with such limited ability to reach things, lift things, understand things, and in general, do a good job. I love my seven-year-old, but I know full well if I hired him to paint my house it would look, well, like a seven-year-old did it.

But back to the point—Jack is hyper-focused on making money and also happens to be incredibly good at making and setting traps with consistency. I feel we've made the right move in hiring him as an exterminator.

May 18, 2021

I have purchased some new supplies for Jack to begin his counterassault in earnest. Mouse attractant, two new varieties of mouse trap (reusable, but deadly), several very large rat sticky traps, and a small live trap that catches animals as large as a grey squirrel.

Even without these new tools, Jack has already earned two dollars for the two mice he captured in the bathroom two days ago. We're heading in the right direction.

It was brought to my attention that Nathan made a side deal with Jack regarding rats. Apparently, they are worth more than the dollar a mouse fetches. Nathan told Jack that the rat was his white whale and it would not be possible for a seven-year-old to be smarter than a rat. Therefore, he will pay Jack five dollars for every rat. I think this deal is a mistake, but time will tell. I give Jack's intellect a nine out of ten chance of being superior to a rat.

May 28, 2021

I owe Jack fourteen dollars. I've never been so happy to owe someone money.

May 29, 2021

Jack caught his white whale last night. He spent the wee hours skipping around the house singing about how Nathan owed him five dollars and that he was indeed smarter than a rat. Nathan woke to this hubbub and while it was earlier than he would have liked, he shared in some of Jack's enthusiasm.

It is, after all, a good thing to be eliminating rats from our basement.

The two of them packed the live trap into the van and headed out to release the poor thing, which was experiencing some distress from having been cooped up all night in the cage. Nathan and Jack were gone for about fifteen minutes. When they returned, Jack came back into the house with less pep in his step than I would have expected. He looked me straight in the eye and admitted that he was not smarter than a rat.

The story came out in one long ranting confession. He and Nathan had gone to our rodent release site, which is nearly four miles from home to prevent re-entry. They had gotten out of the van, walked a few paces, and opened the live trap so that the rat might scurry away. Instead, the rat did the unthinkable. It turned 180 degrees and ran right between the two of them and jumped into the van.

What were they to do but drive home, in utter shock and disbelief? They had been outsmarted fair and square. Jack was extremely agitated by the whole situation. Did it mean he wouldn't get his payout? It wasn't his fault the thing had hitched a ride back home.

Nathan and I will have to discuss the specifics of this particular situation and get back to our exterminator. I don't want bad blood between us and our only hope of eliminating rodents from the house.

The battle continues, as it always will.

Today on the Farm: Mama is Mad

Dani called me this morning at 7:45. She calls me almost every morning, or I call her. This is the first time in my adult life I have had a friend that I talk to every day. It can feel impossible to make friends as an adult. I've always found it strange trying to worm my way into the heart of a complete stranger. And maybe that last sentence makes it clear that I am not particularly good at it. I suppose most normal people wouldn't consider meeting someone new and getting to know them as "worming their way" anywhere.

Dani and I became friends through motherhood. She is a midwife and has now helped bring two of my children into the world. I love her for a million little reasons. She laughs easily and cries easily. She listens to me without judgment, shares her thoughts and feelings without filter, trusting they are safe with me. They are. She listens to me, acknowledges my struggles even though she is also struggling. Dani and I are never competing. Instead, we are always working to hold one another up. But Dani is more than a close friend. She has become part of this family. On the night Ezra was born, Dani held his lifeless body in her warm hands and gave everything she had to save him. Sometimes friends like your children, sometimes they just tolerate them because they like you. Neither is the case with Dani. There is no doubt in my mind that Dani loves my children. She has been bonded to them since their first breaths, and I have never taken this gift for granted.

Dani doesn't care that I'm a little weird. When we talk on the phone, our calls are never entirely pleasant. Not because we're poor conversationalists, but because in the background, our kids scream for food, or for water, or because they have been slighted or are injured. Sometimes we have to pause to address these screams, but often, we continue chatting over them. Between the two of us, we have seven children. We are both working part-time jobs, managing our households, caring for kids, and have hobbies we hope will make us money. When she called, I was relieved to finally have a sympathetic ear. You see, Dani and I are both married to men who leave the car keys in the pockets of their pants when they toss them in the hamper. They are both also men who say things like, "Why didn't you check the pockets before doing the laundry?"

I knew she would commiserate, grunt her lack of surprise at my appalling discovery in yesterday's laundry. Not one, but two sets of electronic keys had been left in Nathan's pockets. The prospect of having to replace these things sent me into a very dark place.

The one good thing to come out of the incident was an interaction with Oggie, who walked into the laundry room just as I was discovering the soggy keys at the bottom of the washing barrel. He could tell I was upset. "What's wrong Mama?"

"I am having a hard time remaining calm, Oggie. I just found two sets of keys that might be ruined and I kind of want to scream."

"You can stomp your feet when you're mad, Mama."

This is advice I have given before when the sound of children screaming has driven me crazy. I like to give options instead of just asking them to stop doing something, especially when they're trying to express an emotion. Mad? Stomp, shake fists in the air, walk away. Frustrated? Growl, use your words, walk away.

For effect, and to confirm that I believed in my own advice, I did some stomping and growling. Oggie seemed pleased that my emotional disruption had been handled. He walked away grinning. "Good job, Mama."

He was genuinely delighted he had helped take care of me. So was I.

As I had anticipated, Dani was empathetic about the keys situation. She and I have the same Toyota Sienna and we have now both washed our keys on multiple occasions. We have also both had our children shove rocks into the sliding door mechanism, thereby destroying it. In many ways, Dani and I are living parallel lives. Our husbands have similar dispositions, making it extremely pleasant to both complain and brag about them to one another. Our kids are of similar ages, so we share concerns, annoyances, and joys. We are both deeply committed to being the best mothers we can be. On the days that I need more than a three-year-old to straighten out my attitude, I am grateful to have Dani.

The Art of the Bench

For the last three years, I have had a secret second job. Most people might be hesitant to classify what I am about to describe as a job. More accurately, I suppose, I have a side hustle. It requires almost no effort and if I had to estimate a monthly time commitment it might average three minutes. Without divulging too much, or sounding like an advertisement, I feel compelled to share this portion of my curriculum vitae. If for no other reason, to encourage others to take three minutes to inadvertently apply for the same job. My second job has been the source of many an eye roll in this house, and perhaps some jealously in my close circle of friends and family. I can only speculate about the latter.

When I buy something on the Internet, I write a review if I love the object, hate the object, or am offered the possibility of some kind of reward for doing so. I write reviews with humor if it is warranted, and sometimes horrific detail. I assume people want both the truth and to be entertained. I start with this disclosure because it is the very act of leaving reviews that started me down this particular path of employment.

My company sells many things. Mostly furniture, but also things like lightbulbs and silverware and water pumps. The items are always changing, and the quality of the items is pretty variable. My company "hired" me because I wrote some candid reviews after purchasing 8 to 10 items from their website. People hit the little thumbs up button more often than not after reading my reviews. I can't say for sure why. Maybe they were funny. Maybe they were helpful. Maybe people are so used to hitting the thumbs up button on social media it was done without much thought. Regardless, my reviews got lots of thumbs ups. The company saw this as proof that my reviews were helping buyers buy. So they "hired" me to write reviews. Honest ones. I can tell you that I am honest. I have given one-star reviews and five-star reviews and I haven't been fired.

You may have noticed I placed the word *hired* in quotations and that is for a very good reason. To hire someone usually requires an interview, a discussion regarding policies and requirements. It usually means that person has applied for a job. In this case, I received an email from the company that looked exactly like spam. I deleted it the first time it came, thinking it was an absurd ploy to get me to engage in accidental password sharing or credit card fraud. The second time the email came, I took a closer look and discovered that the offer was legitimate. I had never heard of such a job, but it was honestly almost too good to be true.

The company wanted me to write more reviews. To do that, they were offering to provide me with items from their inventory. And they were offering to do so every month, for free. At the start of each month, a list of between 200 and 8,000 items was shared with me and I was directed to choose two. Those things were immediately sent and each month I am bound to explain how they are good or bad.

Here is where we come to the eye rolls. Prior to this job, I had, in my life, purchased one bench. It was metal and topped with a lovely swirled cushion. Since taking this job, our house has become filled with benches. Completely unintentionally, I might add. I had no idea I was drawn so powerfully to the bench. They can be wooden (five stars), metal (four stars), or foam (two stars). I apparently love them deeply because it has become an impulsive, "I'll take that one!" when choosing my items. Sometimes benches aren't offered, and this is an equally serious problem (according to Nathan) because when benches aren't on the monthly list, I tend toward extremely large pieces of furniture that inevitably require assembly. The worst of these items (one star) was a TV stand that had bags full of hardware labeled all the way from A to GGG. If that doesn't make sense to you, you probably haven't assembled much furniture and I commend you. But let me explain. If there are 27 separate bags of hardware for an item's assembly, you would likely see a bag labeled with every letter of the alphabet and when the letters ran out at Z, they start fresh with AA.

GGG meant there were 59 individual and unique pieces or kinds of pieces of hardware. I think assembling that TV stand was the day Nathan stopped appreciating my second job. We had to work together for almost three hours while the children destroyed the rest of the house to get the thing together and in the end, it was missing a critical part which made the door inoperable (no returns).

I still very much enjoy my second job. But I will admit that for a short time, while our addition was being constructed and we had to consolidate to live in a smaller section of the house, we were drowning in benches and despite this, I could not help myself. Wrap around bench, (three star), high leg bench (four star). On non-bench months, bunk bed (two star), 8×10 oriental rug (five star). Nathan was in a near panic as the items piled up. He begged me to choose tiny items. Sheet sets, can openers, whatever I could find that could fit in a drawer and not take up half the living room, which was also serving as a dining room and a pantry.

Please Write Review of: Job as a Reviewer
Please submit at least 250 words to describe your experience as a reviewer.
Please assign a star rating.
(Three stars)

I have written many reviews in my lifetime. Yet, I am also fully aware that this job does not truly have any level of required experience and despite the effort one expends in completing the task, there is no discernible pattern to which reviews will be appreciated and which will not. I am also cognizant that people read reviews and often don't believe the good ones and do believe the bad ones. I take this pattern in human behavior to heart and accept that I carry a great responsibility to be honest, but not overly critical. I have enjoyed my time as a reviewer immensely. It has resulted in acquiring no less than seven benches. But more than the dopamine rush I get from the accumulation of worldly possessions, and despite that this occupation has a negative impact on my husband's blood pressure and the square footage of our living space, I think the greatest joy is being able to prevent someone from buying a complete hunk of crap. I would recommend this job to others, but I do so with a few words of warning. You do have to pay taxes on your income. So, if like me, you have chosen 24 expensive "free" items this year, you may want to let those who share your tax burden know before April 15th so they can mentally prepare.

Autumn Rain

The rain has been falling hard all afternoon. Grey clouds hang heavy just above the tree line. I am in my loft, too distracted by the mud in the driveway to get much done. It looks alive, jumping to meet each next drop, propelled by the one before. These cold rains are bittersweet. A goodbye to the heat of summer, to long blades of grass that tangle naked toes as they tread their way across the lawn. Days will shorten, the morning air becoming too cool for bare feet and diapered babies.

Oggie is sleeping deep, the bean bag chair in the living room wrapping gently around him. Bellamy is singing loudly in the kitchen. I can't hear her words, but I know the tune is the movement of her thoughts from imagination to existence. She sings the voices of paper dolls swaying, dresses sweeping the windowsill. She laughs deep, a new character emerges from the depths of a story we are all just now hearing. She is the voice of anyone who can be imagined. She is the thoughts of a spoon and the wishes of the wind chime hanging above the kitchen bench. I often wonder what it would be like to visit the landscape of Bellamy's internal world, what colors would swirl, what music would be playing?

At night before bed, Bellamy has begun listening to *Alice in Wonderland*. I asked her to describe what was happening, thinking that at five-years-old, she may have missed a thing or two, or need clarification. I should have known better. When she is listening, she is Alice. She is growing and shrinking, laughing with the rabbit, talking nonsense with the Cheshire

Cat. She has been visiting Wonderland since she was born and it turns out, I am the one who has missed a thing or two.

The Bracelet I Wear

Is it natural to wear death like a bracelet? One with charms that tinkle and dance with the motion of days and weeks? The music of the chattering pieces, a collection of goodbyes too painful to let go or hold onto. When I wake in the middle of the night, my babies sleeping around me, there it is at my wrist. I wander with it, in the sleepless planes of imagining.

This year has been a hard one. Loss and grief have slunk too close to the edges of my heart. A nephew gone in the night, a son born near-still, a pandemic raging, these terrors grip a mother by the gut. They twist love to fear and dream to nightmare. I lay here in the dark, asking questions too painful to speak aloud. I do it for these four people, sleeping peacefully in the room with me right now. These four, to whom I am bonded in every conceivable way. How will I exist to nurture them, to hold them up and fill them in the time beyond my time? How will I prove the power of my will to love them even through death?

Can I pull time to my heart and wrap myself in it—bend the very thing that pulls at me, tears us all from our bodies in the end? The answer of course, is yes. I can write. From my soul, I can imagine a fortress of words for these children to stand strong upon and do battle. I can write into forever the nights that Bellamy fell asleep with her warm hands resting gently at my neck, her hot breath at my cheek, easy in, easy out. Her warmth, a tiny body pressed against the night into mine, trusting. Bellamy, whose gentleness takes my breath away, with eyes so big and blue they can see the dark places within us all and like magic, bring them light. Her laugh, an easy release of pleasure, an invitation to live bigger and better than before. This child is from my body and while I would love nothing more than to claim some credit for her creation, she is doing it all on her own. Each day creating a self I know not enough about. Each day growing into beauty. A daughter. I have a daughter! I could scream these words to the world or I could weep them. Pride fills me. Panic fills me. I have a daughter in whom I have placed pieces of myself, a gesture, a phrase, a yearning to know words.

Almost imperceptible, this bracelet's cool metal touches new skin with the movement of memory through mind. A gentle reminder of the need my body has to warm it. I ask into the night: What would our goodbye feel like? What texture of loss would I leave for Bellamy to rest her warm hands against? I hope it would be this: a summer morning. We are sitting together on the back steps, looking out at birds fluttering for their breakfasts, listening to the grass as it stretches the dew from its dips and grooves. We are two women, one old and one young, being quiet together—learning to be at peace. Her eyes look up to mine and we smile. Our hearts are full of each other, and of the beauty of this world we love so much. She leans her head onto my shoulder, looks out into tomorrow. Sometimes she is with me. Sometimes she is moving into her own greatness without me. This is the way it should be. The way I know I have done something right.

Her body relaxes around what she knows to be true. She is loved beyond all reason, beyond words and deeds into eternity. I kiss her hair, feeling the warmth of her radiating.

This moment, like every other moment I've ever spent with her, I want to keep. I want to stay right here, holding her, protecting her from a world she does not yet have the need to know. But she is made of iron and rainbow. She gets up, spotting a flower in the upper field, purple against the green. She must pick it. She must tell its story to the wind. She races away, and just like that, the goodbye has happened. Our bodies have said it without ceremony—because they are bodies. They know only motion.

Our hearts though, they don't have to say anything at all. They are one.

~

For Jack, I don't think there is any heartbreak I could willingly give. For all of his strengths, he is also weak in all the right places. When he was just three years old, he would ask me to fall asleep with him. Laying in the darkness, he would share with me his fears and hurts. Shared secret pain, confusion, and joy. We were bonded in our vulnerability. With Jack, I am bare bones and a walking heart. I make mistakes and I tell him I'm sorry for being less than he deserves. This is humanity. This is what I hope I leave him with. A willingness to be naked before his own flaws and whole, despite them. I will carry his humanity if he will carry mine.

We are people together, he and I.

For Jack, I can write us walking through the hush of winter woods. Dusk has come and gone and our hands are warm as they hold each other through our mittens. Even here, beneath the mittens in a memory, I feel the bracelet slide against my wrist as I watch him. He carries the flashlight, but the moon is doing the real work, lighting our way through the glowing snowscape. We are tracking some animal, a chipmunk, a squirrel, a skunk. It doesn't matter. Our eyes scan for footprints, for sign. At the edge of the light the lantern casts on the back stoop, he pauses. The darkness is deeper out here. It makes him nervous to move past the known into something else. We sit together in the snow, listening. Here is the place I wish to sit with Jack in his heart. The boundary between what is known and what he is summoning the courage to learn. Here is where my love will buoy him, hold him, rest patiently until he is ready. And he will be.

He looks to my eyes with determination to go just a little bit further. I see it in him. He will never stop pushing out, challenging what is, conquering fear. I will never stop holding that mittened hand, feeling the power of him swell into each new discovery, each step into the darkness.

~

Ogden means "Valley of Oaks" and there is a place deep within our 42 acres we used to call "The Oak Grove." The property is decorated with massive oaks, but this one place along the deep groove cut by a natural spring was a collection of giant trees we noticed on an early walk. We said to ourselves, how beautiful to have a boy whose name is the namesake of this place. To have chosen so aptly the word to describe this being, to bind him to home in language and space. Though it has just come to light that the bark on these massive trees is not oak, instead it is diamonds stacked on diamonds and we are protecting within our rock wall boundaries the eldest ash trees I have ever seen. If this were a different essay, I might delve into how an oak could be mistaken for an ash, how I should have known from the start what we really had—but this is not an essay about trees or things I should have known. Somehow the whole situation seems a perfect metaphor for Ogden. What I thought I knew, what I should have known, what is.

Like our property, this boy is an expanse of uncharted territory, a marvel, magical. In his tender heart we are working hard to protect what is. When Oggie accidentally hurts someone or makes a mistake that incites adult intervention, he says, "That wasn't real." If you look into his golden eyes and see the hurt there, he is right. "Real" is love in this family, and hurt is not an expression his heart is prepared to endure. At three, his body rejects the very notion of sitting with negative emotions. But his rejection is never from a place of uncaring. His heart folds gently over mistakes when guided. His warm hand wraps into mine as we walk together to make apologies and tell siblings he did not mean for them to be hurt. His eyes work to meet theirs as he holds his mistakes out like offerings. This child is brave in love. His ego sits quietly beside him, holding the ache of wanting connection while his heart pushes into the world to seek it.

For Oggie, whose years on this earth are so short, it is hard to think of a goodbye as our hellos have just begun. The world is so big, so wildly out of reach. I cannot imagine missing all the ways he will explore and revel in its beauty. But if a goodbye was forced, I know something about where my soul would meet his.

There is a place in all of us, a moment between what we know we are meant to do and what our complicated lives push us toward. It is a place of stillness before action. A place of deciding. A moment where the subconscious swirls with our deepest motivations. A place we were meant to be soft, to release our egos and rest before we grow into something better than ourselves. So many of us have lost this place in our busy days, our busy minds, our going and going. So many of us have watched as the softness has hardened ever so slightly, then just a little bit more.

Here, in this place, I will stay with Oggie. I will hold his warm hand as he walks toward hurt and lets himself pause in the gentleness of love. I will sit with my own ego, let it hold my mistakes and my wanting. I will stay soft as I watch my son become more.

At night, when the other kids have fallen asleep, but Oggie cannot drift off, I whisper things in his ears that I hope will find their way to that quiet space within him. I whisper that I am proud and lucky to be his mother. That his heart is big, that his laugh brings light to the world. I tell him he is loved from the forever and into the forever. That is the truth as I know it. A flowing of love holds this child as he is pulled by currents in oceans I have just begun to understand.

~

Ezra is littler still. A baby whose world is smaller than small. He has only known the walls of this home and the 42 acres we call our own. Has seen no crowds, no oceans, no city parks. He is a pandemic baby whose world is the arms that hold him, the siblings who laugh with him, and the milk that sustains him. He is joyful and oblivious. I wish I could write more about who this child will be—who he is—but right now, he is simply an extension of my heart blossoming into the world. In my imagining of this boy's future, he is sitting with Jack where the light grows dim. He is picking flowers with Bellamy in the sun. He is holding Ogden's warm hand into forgiveness. He is here in this world to love.

I cannot accept the premise of a goodbye to this piece of me. Even when at birth, as his tiny body lay motionless, balanced between life and death, I could not accept it. We came so close to losing him on the day he was born that something inside me shifted.

Ezra took my heart to the precipice and there is no turning back. He is why I am wearing death like a bracelet. Because of Ezra, I will write for all of us. I will search for the words to push back against loss.

Chainsaws and Cherry Burls

The tractor trail that leads to the back of the property dissects our black cherry grove. To each side of the path the trees stand tall, their bark a mess of irregular chunks layered atop and across one another. These trees' outer shell forms a rough armor against insects, animals, and the icy Maine winter. Nathan and I are walking the trails one more time before the seasons change, cleaning up downed branches from a summer of storms. Winter is coming and if we keep things clear, we will be able to cross country ski down to the creek, unhindered.

I have an affection for the wild black cherry tree, whose wood is a ruddy blend of paprika and peach. Our black cherries are scattered widely on the property, but there is a small gathering of these hardwoods that falls almost perfectly atop the center of our parcel of land. Heartwood. Of course, heartwood grows within each species of tree—but it seems too perfect that at the heart of our land grows a family of tree whose deepest arteries are almost as red as my own.

But bulbous growths bloom from the cherry trees' trunks as cancers, appearing both low to the ground and in high notches. They are covered in burls. There is no discernible pattern to these cellulose verrucas other than their choice of host. The burl is a tree's response to stress.

I too have been stressed.

In the last eight years, my body has carried four babies. Thirty-eight months of pregnancy in which I sacrificed energy and comfort to nourish and grow four lives. My body labored to bring these babies into existence. Of the last 96 months, 57 of them (and counting) have been spent nursing a baby. This body, my body, has stretched and changed and given everything. And the nights. Eight years of children calling from their sleep—bad dreams, wet sheets, teething, fevers.

At a doctor's appointment this week, I was diagnosed with adrenal fatigue. Dizziness upon standing. Pupils so tired they cannot help but dilate. Headaches. Exhaustion. A sickness caused by paying attention. Too much attention. In the night, when my body should be awash in melatonin, it is jolted and jarred and the cortisol flows. I can no longer sleep a full night. I must begin to retrain myself. Eight years of alertness. I feel desperation and the tingle of real danger.

~

The cherry trees carry a physical memory of harder times, infestations, fungal attacks, harsh winters. These are the beginnings of a burl. Each is unique. A twisting of grains. A wrapping of self that cannot fully be explained. A burl is born from vulnerability.

I too have been vulnerable.

Standing half-naked, a discarded placenta beside me, I held my body upright before the line of men, paramedics and police. Their eyes had tears for the agony they had witnessed, but still they stood motionless, unable to break free from the paralysis of trauma. My baby lay blue on the couch and our midwife pushed hard at his chest. I waited outside of myself to hear his tiny lungs pull life from the ether. Ambulances, helicopters and flashing lights. Time was an elastic being stretched and I waited for the snap.

From terror, a burl is born. A moment that threatens to swallow is wrapped in layers of time, it sits untouched until it has hardened, solidified by distance and understanding.

Even now, with four healthy children who are strong, creative, kind, I feel the soft place within myself. It is where worry sleeps, ever ready. It is where I keep my acceptance of heartache that has yet to come.

To love children is to remain always raw, an exquisite vulnerability.

Around my motherhood a burl grows.

~

Doubt, darkness, fear. These are the invaders to a human psyche. In the moment they break through, touch tentacles to nerve, the transformation begins. A heart builds walls within itself to keep the darkness from the light. Pieces of a person are partitioned, encapsulated, protected. They begin to bulge, to layer the grains of time, experience, choice and consequence one atop another atop another.

Last year, shock and sadness pushed me to the floor. Tears fell from my cheeks as Jack stood before me, fear in his eyes. There is nothing to be afraid of, I reassured. Sadness is part of love. Goodbyes are part of life. Nathan called a family meeting so we could explain. I cried and remembered aloud things that made me laugh, which brought more tears. The kids sat with me, held my hands. They asked good questions. What happens when a person dies? Where do they go? Will we see them again?

I answered honestly. No one knows. But here is what I hope.

Hope, faith, spirituality. These are words for how we wrap our grief. How we layer meaning, gently hold our losses so that we may breathe again.

Grief hides within a burl.

~

I cannot bear to see Nathan cut down these deformed trees. He walks the tractor paths with chainsaw in hand, pointing to this cherry or that. They are too close, he says, the path too narrow. But I argue until he is tired, until he moves ahead to more trail that needs tending. I stay behind, admiring the strength of these trees. None stopped growing. None gave in to the weight of a burl. Instead, they grew bark to protect these swelling hurts. They moved on, waited for time to transform their pain.

I have caused pain. I have been callous and self-centered. Friendships and loves lost because I refused or was incapable of making room for anyone but myself. Time has shown me these failings, has shifted my focus and uprooted a shame I should have long ago addressed.

For each moment in my life that brings regret, a burl grows.

~

In the woodworking world, a burl is a treasure. A living geode, ready to be cracked, shaped, crafted into more. Of course, they aren't all worth harvesting. Some are knots of stained and rotten wood, or so big they cannot be maneuvered or shaped. There is no way of knowing what lies within these misshapen knobs. Some are very likely decayed at their core. Even knowing this, I cannot bring myself to concede a single burl from the heart of our land. Who am I to cull the evidence of such struggle? To guess at which tree has crafted beauty from pain and which has let it fester.

But within myself, I recognize it is my responsibility to curate. I am the wielder of the metaphorical chainsaw—the one who gets to choose which pieces of a past are worth keeping and which are merely deadweight. When we keep a burl, we are acknowledging that growth of cells—of self—within them is uncontrolled. There is risk, but also beauty to the wildness of their expansion.

For each story I cannot yet bring myself to tell, a burl grows.

Each essay put into the world, a window to a burl.

I write because I am driven to cut into these growths in search of art—to examine an inner self as it wraps and twists and swells.

There is tenderness at the core of these malignancies. A soft place we have hidden for when we are strong enough, brave enough, to touch it or maybe to let it go.

~

I hear the chainsaw up ahead. The sound of branches falling, trees being cleared. Likely, some of the trees Nathan is cutting are covered with burls. Spruce, hemlock, pine. For some reason, these losses don't bother me quite as much. They are not so close to a heart. I should join him in the work. Yet, I also know that maybe I shouldn't. I have the habit of fighting to keep trees that hinder the plans we have for using the land. Necessary or not, I am saddened by each loss. Nathan is restricted by no such sentimentality. In the forest, he is pragmatic, systematic, focused on function over aesthetic.

I will wait here. When Nathan tires, he will find me on his walk toward home. For now, standing between these cherries I too am a tree. I am a being with burls.

Bellamy's Raccoon

The Palermo Town Office put out an email about a week ago indicating a positive rabies test had come back for a raccoon in the area. We are all to be on high alert with our dogs and our children. Out here, at any given home, it's hard to say who is the more likely of the two species to have an altercation with one of these wily tree dwellers. It's children in our case. I can't say it has always been this way, but we've recently adopted an electronic fence to keep Tulip from chasing mailmen and terrifying pedestrians of all varieties, which she was doing on an embarrassingly regular basis. This has reduced her territory to a 900-foot radius in the backyard. I wish it didn't have to be this way, but despite the highest quality liver treats and the most affectionate positive reinforcement, she could not be convinced to give up her poor habits. With an electronic fence and some effective training sessions, she now seems extremely uninterested in chasing motorized vehicles and is desperately in need of therapy to sort out her feelings about this new arrangement. All of this is to say, she cannot aimlessly wander, nor can she pick up the scent of a coon and follow it beyond the backyard. The kids on the other hand, are free to roam much further into the property and very well might stumble upon a rabid raccoon.

I brought the concern to Bellamy and Jack while they were playing outside. They had never heard of rabies. I did an overall poor job explaining why a raccoon with rabies should worry them. Turns out my understanding of rabies is quite lacking in specificity. My only real experience with the virus is second- or third-hand and involves a bat attack that may or may not have happened in 1985. The incident in question may have been a completely falsified account passed down to my brothers and me as a warning to avoid animals exhibiting odd behavior.

After I'd done my best to express the dangers of this virus and more generally of raccoons in daylight, Jack informed me that Bellamy had seen a raccoon in the woodpile mere hours before. On average, I would say the kids are about 40% accurate when it comes to reporting pretty much anything. Who hurt who, who saw what, who did what. It doesn't matter what we're talking about. No one agrees on the specifics and its almost always understood and reported differently by all three speaking children. Therefore, I was not particularly concerned that a raccoon had been sighted. There was a 60% chance that a raccoon had not been sighted.

Even with a 40% chance of a raccoon on the premises, I was only about 5% sure we should do something about it. The logical next step to removing a raccoon would be to borrow my father's live trap again. This family is well aware of how one thing leads to another and then that thing leads to a skunk.

When questioned about the raccoon in the woodpile, Bellamy sheepishly mentioned that she'd gotten a speck of dust in her eye and when she glanced about, it looked like a small black shape was zipping through her line of sight. Overhearing this, Jack was appalled. Had there been a raccoon or hadn't there? Bellamy seemed irritated by his fixation with a raccoon when her eye was clearly hurting her.

I am absolutely delighted that Jack and Bellamy are completely opposite in almost every way. If you imagine a spectrum on which human beings exist, Jack would be at the end where there is black and white and true and false and what did and didn't happen. Bellamy would be on the end where a speck of dust in her eye is reported confidently as a raccoon popping its head in and out of a hole in the woodpile. For her, a speck of dust might as well be something more interesting. For Jack, this twisting of reality is completely unacceptable and is also often taken as a personal affront.

I don't have the time to sort out every speck of dust, nor do I believe it is particularly important to do so. I like to leave some mysteries for the kids to work out on their own. Bellamy's imaginative frivolity brings a much-needed balance to the household dynamic. It does us all some good to live with a little uncertainty. In any case, the children were effectively warned to avoid close contact with raccoons, especially ones with frothy mouths.

Since the raccoon was seen or not seen in our woodpile, I haven't been able to stop thinking about how Bellamy moves through the world. I am simultaneously wildly jealous of and also mildly concerned about how she can navigate daily life with such graceful disconnect. She is a storyteller by nature, this much is clear. But Bellamy's take on this pastime is more nuanced than simply telling or retelling what happened. Where most storytellers are either telling their own stories, someone else's stories, or making up a story, Bellamy is not constrained to those three choices. She is often telling her own life story *while* she is living it and the stories do not always reflect the reality of what is actually happening.

When Bellamy began dance lessons as a three-year-old, she hated them. I was there. I saw her act withdrawn and annoyed at the instructor's demands. She did not participate in the activities and had no interest in following the other girls and boys as they pranced around the room. After the first two weeks, I was certain we should stop paying for these classes. I mentioned to Bellamy that she did not have to go anymore if she didn't want to. She was horror-struck. "But Mama, I love dance class!"

Obviously, I was confused by this, as I had not seen one indication of fun, let alone love.

"But you never do any of the dances. It doesn't seem like you want to be there. You *do* want to be there?" I asked this question trying hard to hide my incredulity.

"Mama, here is what we learned," she offered, as she began to dance around the living room like a ballerina. I stared in shock. She knew all of the moves they'd been trying to get her to do for the last few weeks.

"Bellamy, what is the best part about dance class?" I asked, certain she'd find nothing positive to say as I hadn't seen her crack a smile at one of these functions since we'd started. She thought for a minute.

"I think when Katherine and I do twirls together is the most fun. And when Miss Martin does the animal dance and we all laugh and run away."

Here's the thing. Bellamy had never done twirls with Katherine and whenever her instructor Miss Martin did the animal dance, Bellamy hugged my leg and refused to let go. But that's not how Bellamy remembered dance class. In her mind, as she watched the other girls and boys, she'd imagined herself with them, having fun. She'd imagined laughing with Katherine and joyfully evading her teacher. She told herself the story of how she was having fun with these people while NOT having fun with these people. When class was done each week, she chose to remember the fun. Part of me has a hard time condoning this version of dance class because this is not actually what happened in dance class. But maybe we are all just remembering our own versions of ourselves existing in the world.

Maybe we could all use a little infusion of this energy. A refusal to accept our fears, our inability to connect when all we really want is connection. At the end of the day, week, or year, Bellamy will remember being happy. She'll remember being a part of things, being loved by her friends. I hope these stories will give her the confidence to go out into the world and make more.

This year, Bellamy started school. She had never been away from us for more than a few hours and had never experienced any form of schooling. I was obviously worried she might have a hard time with the transition. As I picked up her and Jack after their first day, it became immediately clear that my concerns had been needless. As soon as Bellamy's mask was pulled from her face, she experienced a rupture of enthusiasm so great she could barely fasten her buckles. Her body shook with excitement as she told us about her new friend and mused that one of the kids in her class was named Hulk. She spouted off a hundred more facts about her day: The teacher had helped her fix her ponytail. The boys were mostly well behaved, except sometimes Hulk didn't listen. The kids held their crayons in their fists like knives instead of crayons. Recess was great. They had a picnic with their snacks. The teacher forgot to teach them about letters. There were wooden apples in the class. They did yoga. They watched a TV show while they ate lunch.

Jack and I listened quietly as Bellamy went on and on excitedly. Our eyes met in the rearview mirror and I could tell he was as hesitant as I was to count all of these stories as credible. But the positive energy in the car was infectious. It was impossible not to be swept along in Bellamy's joyful explosion of information.

When we got home, Jack took me aside and asked if there was really a boy in Bellamy's class named Hulk. I shrugged my shoulders noncommittally. We both chuckled.

If you ask her, I have no doubt that Bellamy would tell you all about the friendships she has already formed, the antics of her new superhero classmates, the fun they are all having together. She might also tell you about the rush of adrenaline that accompanies a rabid raccoon sighting.

Tulip Petunia

Tulip Petunia makes my life harder. But sitting here, I can't bring myself to write a single disparaging word about our dog. The reason? I know enough about dogs to understand that my complaints are a reflection of me, not my domesticated coyote. Tulip is an animal. She is not having a hard morning. *I* am having a hard morning. I forgot the breakfast sausages on the table while I changed a diaper in the other room and Tulip ate them. This is my fault, obviously. But how easy it is to be frustrated with the dog who won't act like a human.

I know that complaining about how Tulip does this or that is an attempt to shift the hardness of life right now to a creature who can barely get out of her own way. Weighing in at nearly 80 pounds, Tulip is not a small dog. Her full coat of chocolate fur and extraordinarily fluffy eyebrows make her appear a good ten pounds heavier than that. When I found her in a local ad three years ago, she was so tiny and sweet looking. I thought she would grow to be a great addition to the family, a protector, a guardian. In reality, her defensive tendencies would best be described as completely unnecessary and wildly disconnected from the level of threat. I had no idea that her poodle lineage would prove so difficult to manage. I am trying to remember to breathe through these moments, place my frustration elsewhere.

But life is *so* hard right now.

The living room is covered in playing cards. Cards from decks that should never have met are mingling in piles and pools and clumps. Cards with robots on their faces, with characters from Dr. Seuss books, with numbers and letters and trivia questions. An unsupervised someone, likely the youngest of our crew, has strewn these cards from a box in the game closet.

The dining room floor is another world of chaos. Matchbox cars in lines, crashing into each other, into walls and table legs. They litter the wooden floorboards, miniature munitions at the ready to puncture the delicate skin between toes, at arches, and on tender pads.

Kitchen messes are also abundant. Yes, dirty dishes. But also Legos. A rainbow of agony carried from the playroom, these bulbous foot-busters have taken root, another assault on parental mobility. Each room, another mess. This house is bursting at the seams with the evidence of play. Perhaps also evidence of poor supervision and a lack of adult guidance. I take full responsibility. It is a weekend and in the brief moments I have taken to enjoy coffee with Nathan, the children have overrun us.

I have accepted that we are outnumbered.

But there is more to it than that. In moments of accelerating entropic decay, Tulip is a wildcard in this family. She rides the wave of household deterioration with equal parts joy and confusion. She takes it one step further. For me, her antics are often the final push—the thing that causes a complete mental breakdown.

Tulip's origins are hazy at best, though I do believe I am justified in suspecting a genetic predisposition toward crippling anxiety somewhere in her family tree. By some awful twist in fate, this trait was not only passed down, but also amplified within her. Tulip gets nervous when you open the door to let her outside. Tulip is suspicious of her food bowl. She gets irritated when you throw something in the garbage. In moments of anxiety, she steals toys from the kids' hands, knocks them over with her huge brown body, licks their eyeballs and makes them squeal. When you ask her to calm down, she bounces higher, runs faster, plays harder. When you drink coffee in her presence, she puts her nose under your cup and lifts up with such force that the cup is thrown upward, ripped from your fingers.

After stealing the sausages, Tulip saw the look on my face and knew I was disappointed, though it was unlikely she knew why. She trotted gaily from the room, only to slip on a pile of cards. This caused her to panic, as though someone had pushed her. She threw her head around, looking for the assailant only to find her tail, which she then attacked with enthusiastic growling. While biting at her tail, she bumped Bellamy into a wall. Bellamy admonished her for being careless and at the sound of her name, Tulip bounced high, then landed in play pose facing Bellamy. Her back paw landed on a Lego and slid again, this time into the kitchen. She was then riled. Her body ran circles around the kitchen island, knocking Oggie back into the cabinet. He began to cry. Ezra saw the chaos building and backed away, looking wildly for the arms of an adult to scoop him out of harm's way. If the messes aren't enough to break us, Tulip's inability to navigate them certainly is.

Tulip runs when she should walk. Barks when she should be quiet. She accidentally locks herself in Ally's room about eight times a day. This strange creature is terrified of wind, thunder, darkness, and stuffed pink bunnies.

Tulip is not what I imagined when I daydreamed the perfect pet for this family. She is complicated and irksome and psychologically unstable. But, listen to this. When Ezra needs to get onto the couch and accidentally (or purposefully) steps on Tulip's face to boost himself up, she remains perfectly still until he is safe. When one of the kids is scared of the dark and calls Tulip to sleep in their room, she stays until they are breathing slow and deep. When Oggie accidentally falls and his elbow pinches Tulip's ear to the floor, she does not nip him. She puts her nose to his as if to ask if he is OK. Tulip lets Jack wrap her in hugs and cover her with blankets. She rests her head on his pillow while he curls his body into hers on cold winter mornings. Tulip sits quietly at Bellamy's feet when she is singing loudly with paper dolls flailing wildly through the air.

I have certain family members who see our life and ask why we have chosen to keep such a complicated dog when our lives are complicated enough without her. Of course, they are right that things would be simpler without a dog. But what is the fun in seeking simplicity? My hope is that eventually I will reach a place of Zen where sausage theft and untimely excitement cause me to laugh instead of scream. And I hope that Tulip will forgive me for how long it takes to get there, because I've still a good distance to go.

Going Home

Seasickness is a body speaking its discomfort. Sometimes it is a quiet whisper, nausea wetting the lips, a tingling in the head. Other times it is a scream so violent it sends us to the railing, clutching our guts as we are twisted in pain. "Too much," the body says. "I cannot go from stillness to the sway of these waves." Homesickness too, is a body speaking. "I am yearning," the body says. "My heart aches for home and yet I am helpless as time sweeps me away." For seasickness there are pills to take and body movements to slow its spread, but how does one combat the melancholy of missing home? What is the treatment to alleviate yearning? In the battle against homesickness, science puts down her beaker and leaves the lab. In this fight, we are alone.

When I was seven or eight, I was invited to friends' houses for sleepovers on Friday or Saturday nights. I loved the idea of spending time with them outside of school and always accepted these invitations. As the evening wore on, there was the inevitable moment of reflection, games were put away and meals finished and in the quiet of someone else's home, in the silence of my own mind, a call would come. An urging, painful almost, to my small body. It was the sound of my mother's voice saying goodnight to my brothers, but not me. Our family's green plaid couch, armrests worn bare, with no one to lay a sleepy head upon them. The empty bed in my room, down covers pulled back, pillows askew. An assault of ,"You are missing." And I was. I was aching to place myself back into the void of my own absence. How strange and how seemingly impossible to cure.

~

Home is where the heart is.

This is what we tell ourselves to dull the sting of leaving one place for another. The implication is that our home is merely a manifestation of our feelings of belonging to other people, that our family is all we need to feel complete. To move is not to leave home, but to take home with you. But there is this: my heart has entire chambers filled with Maine wildflowers. The smooth silk of pink and blue petals. The way our lilac's fragrance hangs thick on a spring breeze as it passes beneath the maples, mingling with the earthy musk of soil after an afternoon rain. The delicate bowing of an eastern red columbine stem, the waxy purple of a jack in the pulpit, the exuberance of a wild aster, petals flailing.

I am about to describe all of the ways in which home is not about family, but it is mostly about them. It is the place where each of us are our best because each of us is comfortable being exactly who we are. I am privileged to feel this way. I grew up in a loving home. Was part of a farming family. I had jobs and responsibilities and this usefulness was a constant infusion of value, an affirmation of self-worth. You belong here because you are needed here and we are a team. You belong here because when you are gone, things are harder. You are missed. This is not to say that my belonging was transactional or impersonal, but for me, the importance of shared goals and common purpose cannot be overlooked. The people who love us and are loved by us should not be under-appreciated.

What I am trying to say is that home is more than the people who fill it. Our hearts are big and complicated. They have room enough for flowers and soil, wind and thunderstorms, bean fields and mountains. There are always chambers yet to be filled.

~

Last week I was on vacation with Nathan and the kids in Vermont. This is where Nathan's family is from, and on sunny afternoons we gathered on the deck of his father's camp at the foot of Mt. Elmore. Nathan and the kids enjoyed the company of his extended family, their voices loud and jubilant at the lake's edge. I love Nathan's family deeply. They are an assortment of intellectual and psychological wonders. Mathematicians, musicians, engineers, nuclear physicists, lawyers, potters, researchers, goofballs. They are some of the most beautiful and authentically kind and giving people I have ever met. But, on the upper deck of a camp that was not mine, I felt alone. Homesick. Our first few nights in Vermont, Oggie had trouble falling asleep. "When will we go home?" he asked. "Why do we have to sleep here? Can we sleep in the car and drive home?"

Bellamy grew upset hearing her brother talk about home. "I want to be in our own house too," she complained. "I miss playing under my tree."

Unintentionally, I began to carry within myself the homesickness my children felt as well as my own yearning for home. I was hearing the call as loud as I ever had, and there was no kayak trip or swim in the lake's cool waters that would work to quiet it.

There are chambers of my heart filled with the shadow-shapes cast by rustling leaves on the hillside in the backyard. The movement of wind and leaves performing a dance of right here, right now. But I was not right there. I was in

Vermont and my heart was heavy holding the emptiness where my body might have been to take it all in.

The day after the children expressed their longing for home, Mt. Elmore saddened me. I was floating without ground—the ground I knew, to pull at me toward calm, slow my thoughts, listen. There, the lawn clippings smelled too much like gasoline and not enough like lemon clover. The air tasted like mud, the scent of lake vegetation coated my nostrils and throat. I only saw one bird. The family gathering was unable to fill the space I was carrying for myself and my kids because the only ones that could fill that space were us. But not there.

The clouds were really moving. Mt. Elmore stood across the lake watching them pass between us. If she were my mountain, she would know well the weight of my footsteps and I would know her trees and mushrooms and walking trails. I would know the view from the top and up there I would feel both familiar and at peace with myself and the breath required to make the climb. There is no loneliness in the nature of home. Some would argue that's all there is, but this is the seed of the sickness my kids and I were fighting. To know land, to be known by land, is to be seen by ourselves with no filter. It is to exist in the silence of a second and then another and then another without looking forward or back.

The mountain does not judge how fast the climb or how effortless. The mountain feels the soles of your feet and knows only that you are moving. If she is your mountain, she will also show you yourself. But that mountain was not my mountain. She was beautiful, no arguing that, but she did not ease yearning in my heart. Instead, the call's echo reverberated across the lake and filled my chest with, "You are missing."

~

Wars are fought over what land is whose home. There are homelands and homecomings and when we are tired, we head homeward. Nathan does not feel the same way about home. He is not tied to a specific place, has never felt homesick when visiting his friends as a child. If I didn't know this to be true, I would doubt it could be possible. How can someone not link themselves with the land, with the place they are meant to be? But maybe he is doing something right that I have never learned to do. He can appreciate the breeze in Vermont and in California and in Maine. He can smell flowers in South Carolina as easily as in our own backyard and they are no less sweet. He can fall asleep in a soft bed that is offered to him without imagining his own, empty and longing for him.

Despite my brain telling me he might be on to something, my heart cannot help but find his flexibility deeply unsettling.

~

Here are some things I know about our 42 acres:

The color of sunrise. Over the pond, the pink glow of daybreak catches my breath. No matter how many times I see it. Like spilled paint, it spreads in waves, shifting color as it pushes back the darkness. I know the pond water's temperature as summer slides into fall or spring to summer. I know the trees that house porcupines and the ones at risk of meeting a beaver's teeth. When one of my children has walked through the mint, the scent swirls through open windows and clings to dirty toes as they continue their play.

Our land does not stand stiff and cold when we walk. She bends each blade of grass to cup our feelings like a friend who does not have to say, "I am listening" because it has never been any other way.

~

During our visit in Vermont, we went on a drive through the mountains in Stowe. Nathan began musing about the geology, how Vermont and neighboring states had once been on separate continental plates. This idea appealed to me—that I had transitioned to another landmass altogether. That the land itself was moving beneath me. Maybe such an extreme change in location (a new continent!) was exacerbating my homesickness.

I suppose no matter what rocks crashed into which and when, there is only one nature. This land is connected to that land which is connected to the land beside that. But there is only one place that I can tell you where the sparrows make their nests each spring. On our land, in Palermo, Maine, I can show you where the first tulip will pop from the soil to test its luck with the spring air. I know where the low bush blueberries will ripen first, and which trees have wild chestnuts dangling beneath their broad leaves.

~

I wasn't homesick all of the time, but much like seasickness, my homesickness came in waves. Strongest the first few days away from home, as my body adjusted to its new surroundings. Then it came more sporadically and was dependent on other things, like how tired I was, or how busy.

A week into the trip, I found myself sitting alone on the deck of a cabin, listening to others laughing into a summer breeze, wishing for a different summer breeze that smelled a little more like apple blossoms and lemon clover. Admittedly, it was a bit ridiculous. To yearn is to stop seeing what is here and imagining somewhere else. Too much yearning and we cannot live full lives. For this reason, I make an effort to allow only short bouts of it before pulling myself back to the present.

I shared my thoughts with Nathan's family over the dinner table and was not completely surprised to learn that almost none of them experience homesickness like I do. They wondered if I wasn't confusing nostalgia for this feeling of loss or missing out. Maybe nostalgia plays a small role, but I argued that I was not homesick for my childhood home in Freedom, Maine. I am nostalgic for the memories I made there, but that, I explained, was not the same thing as homesickness.

~

As if the universe was calling me to defend (or maybe confront) my distinction between homesickness and nostalgia, an unlikely opportunity arose not long after returning home from the Vermont trip. I was asked to join a friend on a visit to my childhood home, a farm I had not stepped foot on in almost 17 years. I wondered, would that farm tug at me, cause the same discomfort it had the first few years after we left? Would I have to eat my words at the clear separation between places long lost and places alive in our every day?

My friend and I drove to the farm through the back roads of Freedom, traversing Goosepecker Ridge Road to Greeley. As we rounded the hill by the old cemetery, the driveway's rough pavement came into view and the flood of memories began in earnest.

I used to cross the road as a child of seven or eight, to walk down the long clean rows of beans to where the field kissed the woods. Just behind the lush branches of underbrush and bramble lay a quiet place I visited often. It was a dumping ground for boulders pushed up by frost heave each spring and housed gigantic stones situated in what I had always thought a Stonehenge-esqe circle. This and a thousand other reminders of what the land had once been erupted within me. Of course, memories of how our family had lived and loved also surfaced. How my brothers and I had dared one another to jump into the red bull's pen, to goad him into a chase back to the fence with just enough time to dive under it to safety. My mother's flower garden, always overflowing. Riding bikes in endless circles at the top of the drive. Dancing half-naked in the spring rain, mud splashing onto our laughing faces. I loved our farm in Freedom.

But this was not our farm.

I was not homesick walking the old tractor paths or standing beneath the pear tree.

~

My homesickness while in Vermont was a longing for the home I have right now—a home I am actively building, children who are growing and learning to appreciate the nature that surrounds them. But even as I write this, the flowers outside are dying down. The leaves will soon drop from the trees. There is no way to stop the flow of time and so home is also always shifting, ever so slightly, to meet us where we are.

Someday my children will move from our home in Palermo and go out into the world. Maybe they will be like their father, finding beauty in each new place, always present and open to change. Or maybe they will search for a place where leaves whisper the secret of the shifting seasons and flowers hide beside the moss-covered rocks of a gully known only to them.

I don't know if one path is any better than the other. I don't know if the comfort of attachment is worth the pain of eventual loss. Home is a place. For some it moves and changes with dizzying speed, for some it is one slow transition after another. For me, whether I am in the hills of Vermont or sitting beneath the ancient ash and oaks on our land, home is both where I am and where I am going. It is family and it is my heart being bound every day by the ephemeral tendrils of the natural world.

Walking with the new owner through her fields of shallots and garlic, picking a rogue weed as a matter of muscle memory, the land felt different. It *was* different. This was no longer the farm I grew up on. Even though the cement block beneath the machinery shed still held my etched initials, I felt myself fading. Cement was the only thing here that remembered me. The land I knew had been moving away from me as fast as I had been moving away from it. While I could feel nostalgia tightening my chest as we explored the property, I felt no sadness at leaving when the time came.

As we drove away from the farm that afternoon, I imagined the land beneath us as a cresting wave, imagined myself a traveler on the tectonic plates beneath, fluid, yet so impossibly slow on their journeys I hadn't ever noticed they were moving.

Up Here, I Write

The loft is the home's equivalent to a secret pocket.

When I was very young, my parents would take my brothers and me to have dinner with their friends, fellow farmers who lived a few miles away and who had two daughters. The house was unique in that there were holes in places our house didn't have holes. At least, that's how I remember it. There were hiding spots where we could peek from the girls' rooms down into the living room. We would play up there, and when our play soured, we'd eavesdrop on the grownups down below. We could see the tops of their heads and hear their voices without being seen. This is when I first fell in love with the idea of the loft—the feeling of being safely tucked within one.

A loft offers something that no other room can. It is both a part of another space and not. It provides privacy for the occupant while stripping privacy from those down below. While I am generally against stripping privacy from people, I am not opposed to being able to sit at my desk in my loft and still remain within earshot of four small children who are often up to no good.

There is safety and comfort in a loft. It's protected, private, special. This is usually how I feel as I sit at my desk, writing essays or filling out various other paperwork for my day job. But not today. Today I feel vulnerable and alone and very much like a failure. In the living room below me, Ogden is sick with COVID-19. He is sleeping peacefully in the beanbag chair while his siblings, who are also sick, get tested for a second time. The school requires a positive test for each child before they can make certain decisions. Rules. Procedures. Regulations. We are doing our best to follow them. We are doing our best to keep others safe. But the truth is sitting heavy on my chest. We did not do enough to keep our *own* children safe.

Ogden's fever has just now come below 105°, and I am tired, deflated. He is the one I was trying so hard to protect. He is the one who wakes in the night, gasping for breath, sporadic croup closing his airways with the littlest cold. We are only at the beginning of this infection and I am scared and sad and ashamed.

Shame.

What a strange thing to feel about a virus. I have never been ashamed to be sick or to have kids who were sick before. But this is different. We have been careful. We have canceled family functions and been laughed at for our liberal paranoia. This family has made enemies with our choices to stay away.

And here we are.

Sick.

The loft offers no protection from that truth.

~

There was a room in the third floor of my university's library covered in tiny private loft sanctuaries. The ceiling was tall enough to accommodate these miniature elevated cubicles. Each one had a desk, chair, and a small staircase. These cozy caves were my favorite place to study and I would often rush to the library early in the morning to claim one for a long day of research or test prep. They were coveted spots, perfect for maintaining focus while still being surrounded by the hushed voices of fellow students. They were also an escape, a place to hide. From the floor, it was impossible to see who was in which loft cubicle. If you didn't want to be found, you wouldn't be.

In my loft, the pair of leather chairs and the distressed wood of the round table between them make me think of both a coffee shop and a psychiatrist's office. I am pleased with the aesthetic. Though, I'm not sure how the rainbow-colored rug and half-barrel full of blankets and pillows fit in. Perhaps the chaise and the purple poof ottoman are too much. I love them though.

I am protective of this space. It is the only one in the house I can call mine. It is the only one in the house I have decorated with intention. Most of the other rooms are full of furniture we got for free, old hand-me-downs, a mishmash of styles and colors.

It is not the time to be describing my office. The color of my ottoman and the way that I stuff the bookshelves are not important when there are fevers and fear.

But I need a little bit longer.

~

Right now, as I write, I can hear the air moving in and out of Ogden's lungs. If I peek over the edge of my loft office, I can see his flushed cheeks resting against the royal blue velour of the living room chair. He is fine. He will be fine. If I have to, I will bring him into my loft, lay his burning body on my chaise and let him sleep close.

This is not the time to write an essay about COVID-19 or lofts. It is a time to snuggle my babies and kiss their hot skin. It is a time to be a mother. But maybe, for a minute or two more, I can sit here waiting for the feeling to come. To be enveloped, sheltered, whole. A few months ago, I bought a beautiful print at a gift shop of vibrantly colored birds sitting on a line. They are paint splatters of green and violet and fuchsia with long thin beaks and tiny black eyes. I hung the print over my desk, a constant reminder that I am changing, that finding beauty requires an open mind, open eyes. Before these kids and their bird watching, I would never have seen these birds as more than birds.

I have filled this loft with color and comfort. Plush pillows and tufted rugs, secret bars of dark chocolate with chai and hazelnut chunks. On warm days, the loft stays cool, on cold ones, the hot air rises from below and swirls around my bare feet. The windows up here have no curtains, light comes in from both ends, unrestricted, inviting.

My loft is the place where secret presents are hidden, where children come for one more hug and Nathan visits to drink coffee before we start our work days. It is where I find the space to breathe deeply, to reset when anger flares or sadness grips me.

Today the floor is cold on my bare feet and the air is an unwelcome tickle at my neck. I am having a hard time remembering what this loft is supposed to feel like. Soon I will hear Ogden wake, he'll moan for me in his half-sleep, asking for a hug or another blanket. I should go down, drink some water, take a shower. But I'm not ready.

I just need a little bit longer.

Today on the Farm: Seedpod

This morning Bellamy came running into the house with something cupped gently in her hand. "Mama!" she screamed excitedly. "What is this plant called? It explodes when you touch it!" I looked at her small palm that she held open for me. Resting at its center was a green touch-me-not seedpod, fat with seeds. I asked her to show me how it exploded. With a smile on her face she gently picked up the pod and squeezed its center. I remember these from when I was a child. I used to love finding a wild touch-me-not, roughly waving a hand back and forth over its leaves, flowers and pods to watch them snap open and shoot seeds into the air. Bellamy's eyes rose to mine as the pod between her fingers gave a small pop and its contents exploded from her hand. She laughed when the seed struck my nose and my eyes went wide with surprise.

Ever since our walk a few months ago, when I insisted we find fifty different plant species before going inside, she has been curious to know the names of the plants she finds. On that walk, the kids had all assumed it would take us hours to find fifty species of plants. It took us about ten minutes and we didn't have to walk more than a hundred feet into our forest trail to find them. Every step the kids would scream, "What's THIS?" picking a new leaf or flower or fern.

On that walk we found five species of fern: cinnamon fern, Christmas fern, royal fern, sensitive fern, and interrupted fern. Oggie could not contain his amazement. "Ferns have kinds?" We examined the pattern of the leaves together, compared one fern to another, made guesses about what they might be called before looking them up.

Now, when Bellamy plays in the front yard and catches a glimpse of a weed she's never seen, she picks it and brings it to me for identification. I wish I knew them all by heart, but I don't. I'm a beginner at this, just like her. Maybe that's why she enjoys it so much. She can tell we're learning together, figuring out something about our land that neither of us knew before.

What We Leave Behind

Our house and property are usually a complete disaster. The messes appear faster than I can clean them. Despite near constant effort to provide my children with meaningful lessons on accountability and neatness, it hasn't improved in the four years we've lived here. It might have something to do with this family's rate of expansion or the ratio of adults to children. Most days I have the energy to fight the chaos with turbo cleans and multitasking, but on rare occasions I give up for 24 to 36 hours and watch in detached curiosity at how things devolve. It brings me a weird pleasure to imagine that at the height of the decay, a volcano will erupt and cover it all in molten ash, thereby preserving our living conditions for future archeologists. This fantasy began shortly after watching a documentary on Pompeii. It was fascinating to hear the archeologists hypothesize about the lives of the people they uncovered based on a few pots and some art. It was also wildly amusing to imagine them doing the same for us in some distant future. This is obviously a simplification of some really amazing research, but as someone who hasn't slept a full night in roughly 9 years, I don't have the capacity to engage with science like I used to.

In the future documentary of our demise, the researchers would pretty quickly conclude that our house served as both a furniture distribution center and a dangerously understaffed daycare facility. Toys littering the floor of every room coupled with the perplexing number of benches in such a small square footage would leave little wiggle room for any other plausible scenario. It would be painfully obvious to these futuristic archeological looky-loos that in this home, supervision was sorely lacking. As an example, if the volcanic eruption were to happen today, here are the items that would appear on a catalog in no particular order, from the downstairs bathtub: metal forks, toy cow, drone battery, tube of Neosporin, pony figurines, the entire family's toothbrushes, and a small bowl full of cement chunks.

~

The land immediately surrounding the house would indicate rural family with an indeterminate number of children (most likely ten or more) and adults with poor time-management skills. Children's toys of astonishingly variety, skill level, and value all abandoned, likely well before the eruption. Lawn mowers, shovels, pogo sticks, wheelbarrows, and bicycles scattered in impossibly illogical locations, despite the presence of a barn and garage that could easily house them. Kitchen implements such as salad tongs, spatulas, and sushi rolling mats sitting inexplicably (even to me, a person who currently lives here and has on multiple occasions implored the children to stop stealing my utensils) beneath the bird feeder, which is full of petrified chicken feed, not bird-seed.

The deep melodic voice of the lead archeologist would say, in a calm but somewhat baffled voice, "These humans were obviously struggling. It is unclear why, as they appear to be of average socio-economic standing, and there does not appear to have been a food shortage or any particular environmental disruption prior to the volcanic eruption." The camera would pan over the hulls of six bicycles, two scooters, an assortment of construction toys, and a barbie family all encrusted with ash and scattered over the property. "What could have befallen this family? What tragedy remains as of yet undiscovered? What physical or emotional impairment could cause these people to live so seemingly disconnected from order and societal norms?"

Then the camera would zoom slowly toward the barn.

"This style barn was common in farming communities," the voice would go on. "It was typically a structure for housing livestock, storing equipment and food to care for those livestock, and sometimes food storage for the humans who inhabited the land." The video feed would cut to a team of scientists walking through our barn's rubble shaking their heads in disbelief. One of them could be heard muttering, "I haven't found a single indication that animals were kept here. But this appears to be a fairly expensive, (five star) bathroom vanity with granite countertop. And over here, I believe this is a pile of tools, each with a small combustion engine and not one in working condition." A second researcher would chime in, "Why would one family need so many tools with small engines? History books indicate these tools were notoriously difficult to repair."

The confident voice of the lead archeologist would begin to talk again as the camera continued to slide over a truly incomprehensible assortment of items within the barn. "In truth, we cannot begin to understand the complicated lives of every rural family. We may never uncover the reason this family resided on a farm yet lived completely outside of the bounds of our current understanding of this lifestyle. How did they support themselves? What did they eat? Why are there so many rodent traps? These questions, and many more, continue to motivate us to dig deeper, to uncover the hidden lives of these early humans."

~

While the mental gymnastics of scripting this documentary delight me, I should probably acknowledge I am not so keen on imagining my entire family being overtaken by a deluge of molten ash. I doubt that something so spectacular will be our undoing. But an end *will* come. Whether it is here, on Asteroid 23567, or some other plot of land or cloud colony of the future. People exist and then we cease to exist. And for better or worse, we can't help asking ourselves, "Why?"

I have recently become intrigued by the idea that humans are merely a fragment of nature that has become self-aware. That we are not separate from the mayflowers, the wasps, or the chickadees like we think we are. As a species, we are unique in the way that thousands of flowers on the same blossoming apple tree are unique, if one (humans) were aware of the tree's existence. In a universe whose underlying impulse is entropic, it is profoundly mysterious to me that life on Earth fights endlessly to organize, complicate, and push back against decay. I have always appreciated the struggle of the underdog—and how could anyone see the complexity and diversity of living things as anything else? Our connection to every other living thing is a product of billions of years of building, of seeking survival against all odds. As the first self-aware piece of nature, maybe it is our responsibility to notice how impossibly precarious our place here really is.

Is this why I am so drawn to the fragrance of spring, to the ice-covered gurgle of the water as it traces the verdant valley? Why I want my children to spend their time exploring and appreciating, paying attention to flailing asters on the hillside and the shimmers of light as they pass through the leaves of our trees?

But I'm not certain this answers the question, "Why?" If I were to keep it simple, to stick to what I know to be true from watching living things live, the answer to "Why?" and to

"What do we leave behind?" is the same. We leave ourselves and everything that came before us within our children. We can write books and paint paintings and dream. But when we are gone, we live through the next generation and the next and the next. This does not discount the very real and powerful influence of those humans who do not or cannot have children. Their influence also passes to the children born within their spheres. The magic of being human is that our awareness, growth, and potential can be shared beyond the chemical bonds of our genetic material.

~

Thought experiments about volcanic catastrophe aside, when my family is long gone from these 42 acres, the land will likely hold no memory of our passing. But we have the capacity to remember, to be changed and bettered by how we lived here. The memories and lessons learned will differ wildly depending on who is doing the remembering. Maybe Jack will recall the snakes and the worms and the way a soccer ball rolled across the grass. Bellamy might remember the fairy houses tucked in the roots of the maple, the flowers sprouting from beneath the mulberry tree. I imagine Oggie will know well the feel of the wind whipping at his face as his bicycle zoomed from the top field to the road, bursts of adrenaline in a hundred different stunts he has just begun to discover. Ezra will surely remember the pond, splashing, diving, swimming hard to the other side. He is a water baby, even now, at one. Nathan's memory will be full of walks through the orchard, the taste of his first plum, a variety called black ice. And for me, it will be the gentle tickle of a velvety white bell as I bring it to my nose for the first smell of spring.

It is my hope that these children pass to their own a desire to know the shape of the conopid fly's tail and the pattern of spots on the ladybird's back. That they will believe, like I do, these details matter.

To appreciate the natural world is to understand the nature of self. To accept that nothing lasts. Seasons change. Continents shift, flowers drop their petals, each winter the soil grows cold as the frost works its fingers ever deeper. To smell the husk of a fallen beechnut, to feel the flakey bark of an ironwood beneath your fingertips on a summer walk. These are deliberate acts of awareness. They are moments of pleasure tucked within the pocket of time, ever flowing. They are both a gift and the promise of loss.

Acknowledgements

A heartfelt thank you to my family for allowing me the space and time to write these essays. And more, for believing, like I do, that there is value in sharing the stories of our life here on the farm.

My deepest appreciation for the tedious job of editing and fine-tuning goes to my editor, Chelsey Clammer, and my publisher, Patricia Newell from North Country Press. I could not ask for a better team in bringing this work to life.

Lastly, a thank you to Tulip Tree Review for publishing *Battleground* in their 2023 Humor edition.

www.ingramcontent.com/pod-product-compliance
Lightning Source LLC
Chambersburg PA
CBHW030331100526
44592CB00010B/657